D1379001

Cosmic
Karma

About the Author

Marguerite Manning is a freelance writer and practicing astrologer in the Washington, DC, metro area, specializing in karmic astrology. She conducts group seminars on karmic astrology and has been published in *Mountain Astrologer*.

To Write to the Author

If you wish to contact the author or would like more information about this book, please write to the author in care of Llewellyn Worldwide and we will forward your request. Both the author and publisher appreciate hearing from you and learning of your enjoyment of this book and how it has helped you. Llewellyn Worldwide cannot guarantee that every letter written to the author can be answered, but all will be forwarded. Please write to:

Marguerite Manning
℅ Llewellyn Worldwide
2143 Wooddale Drive, Dept. 978-0-7387-1054-9
Woodbury, Minnesota 55125-2989, U.S.A.

Please enclose a self-addressed stamped envelope for reply, or $1.00 to cover costs. If outside the U.S.A., enclose international postal reply coupon.

Many of Llewellyn's authors have websites with additional information and resources. For more information, please visit our website at http://www.llewellyn.com.

Cosmic Karma

Understanding Your Contract with the Universe

Marguerite Manning

THREE RIVERS PUBLIC LIBRARY
25207 W. CHANNON DRIVE
P.O. BOX 300
CHANNAHON, IL 60410-0300

Llewellyn Publications
Woodbury, Minnesota

Cosmic Karma: Understanding Your Contract with the Universe © 2007 by Marguerite Manning. All rights reserved. No part of this book may be used or reproduced in any manner whatsoever, including Internet usage, without written permission from Llewellyn Publications, except in the case of brief quotations embodied in critical articles and reviews.

First Edition
First Printing, 2007

Cover art © ImageZoo
Cover design by Gavin Dayton Duffy
Editing by Connie Hill
Llewellyn is a registered trademark of Llewellyn Worldwide, Ltd.

Library of Congress Cataloging-in-Publication Data
Manning, Marguerite.
Cosmic karma : understanding your contract with the universe / Marguerite Manning. — 1st ed.
p. cm.
ISBN: 978-0-7387-1054-9
1. Astrology. 2. Houses (Astrology). 1. Title.
BF1708.1.M368 2007
133.5—dc 2007009802

Llewellyn Worldwide does not participate in, endorse, or have any authority or responsibility concerning private business transactions between our authors and the public.

All mail addressed to the author is forwarded but the publisher cannot, unless specifically instructed by the author, give out an address or phone number.

Any Internet references contained in this work are current at publication time, but the publisher cannot guarantee that a specific location will continue to be maintained. Please refer to the publisher's website for links to authors' websites and other sources.

Llewellyn Publications
A Division of Llewellyn Worldwide, Ltd.
2143 Wooddale Drive, Dept. 978-0-7387-1054-9
Woodbury, Minnesota 55125-2989, U.S.A.
www.llewellyn.com

Printed in the United States of America

3 1561 00205 9156

Contents

Dedication

To Michael,

I never knew just how bright the stars shone or how lucky mine were, until there was you.

When he shall die,
Take him and cut him out in little stars,
And he will make the face of heaven so fine
That all the world will be in love with night
And pay no worship to the garish sun.

—WILLIAM SHAKESPEARE

Heart and Soulfelt Thanks to

The authentic soul of my father, Joe Vaccacio, for not only living his life without complaint, but for eternally shaping mine with the unconditional faith he had in himself, his country, his God, and the times tables;

the artistic soul of my mother, Dorothy, for all the imagination she ignited while selflessly reading to her own children, and all the creativity she inspired by happily painting with mine;

the enlightened soul of Marge Perrino for being both a shining example of Gemini excellence as well as a brilliant universal reminder that when the student is ready the godmother will always appear;

the passionate soul of John McEntee, who always managed to impact my life with his infinite wisdom, generous spirit, and dynamic energy by somehow never failing to make me feel worthy of them;

and, finally, a very grateful shout out to the cosmos for entrusting me in this lifetime with three of its most promising souls and brilliant energies: Lindsay, my true Polaris, Whitney, my luminous Vega, and Jonathan, my incomparable Sirius. Unquestionably, the three earthly lights of my life.

Introduction

The more I study the universe, the more I am convinced of a Higher Power.

—ALBERT EINSTEIN

If you're one of those people who don't believe that you have a soul, you've got the wrong book in your hands, because *Cosmic Karma* is more than just an astrological guide to the soul—it's an astrological guide *for* the soul. It was written to help the immortal part of you (the part that's lived many times before and will live many times again) become even better at it every time it lives—starting with this time, and, I hope, with this book. This can only occur if you can accept the two most important principles it was based on: first, the spiritual belief that every human being is infinitely connected to a soul; and second, the more scientific theory that each and every soul is infinitely connected to the universe. Why? Because together these two principles paint the bigger spiritual picture that sends the higher astrological message that I subscribe to: there really is a universal pool of power, knowledge, and abundance out there, and it's ours for the taking through the higher consciousness of our soul.

I call it "the cosmos," but you think of it as the "Universal Mind," the "Collective Consciousness," or simply "Creation." Either way, no matter what any of us choose to call this all-knowing, omnipresent energy, most people who acknowledge its existence see it as that supreme state of power and awareness that connects everyone and everything to each other. Many physicists describe it as being always available to all of us, but only accessible to each of us when we're finally able to check our egos at the door and function in total oneness with it. Tough to understand? Well, it's even tougher to live with because that means our universal birthright to prosper through our soul's connection to this powerful and abundant universe actually comes with a disclaimer. Birthright or not, none of us are really connected to the universe if we're not living by the laws and principles that govern it. These are the very same universal principles, by the way, that were not only instilled in the soul when it was created, but were also reflected in the heavens on the day that we came into this world as well—in short, the universal laws of divine order—or as they're more universally known, the principles of *Oneness, Correspondence, Vibration, Polarity, Rhythm, Compensation, and Gender.*

That brings us to the reason this book was written. It is a wake-up call to our sleeping souls, because while we may not have been around for Universal Law 101, our souls were. Therefore, if they don't show up with the spiritual know-how in this lifetime, we'll never live up to the physical promise of this universe. After all, according to Universal Law, when we humans don't live by the order that created us, we're forced to live with the chaos that destroys us—the same chaos that we create when we ignore Universal Law. It is our chaos—and, because of that, our karma.

Okay. So you're not sure you're ready to embrace the concept of karma? Well, think again, because there's a pretty good chance that you already do. That's because there's an even better chance that, like most people, on some level you've already accepted the theory of reincarnation. Don't think so? Well, let's see if you do. To begin with, you can't accept the principles of either karma or reincarnation if you don't believe that you have a soul, and since you have yet to put this book back on the shelf, it's a fairly safe assumption that, at least when it comes to the soul, you're a believer. Now, we'll take it one step further. If you're a person who believes in any kind of heaven, eternal hereafter, or even a spiritual dude ranch where some part of you gets to live on in any way, shape, or form after your death (other than the physical body you were born with in this life), then you may be surprised to learn that you are, in fact, someone who believes in reincarnation. It's true, because any kind of existence for you or your soul after this one, whether it be physical, spiritual, or otherwise, is a rebirth for the soul. That, according to every dictionary I've come across, including *Webster's* and *Oxford American*, is what the word "reincarnation" means. Nothing more. But go ahead, look it up, you'll feel better.

And while you're there, save yourself another trip and look up the word "karma." As you'll see, this is an ancient Hindu word that means inevitable fate or self-decided destiny. It snuck into our modern-day vocabulary through the older spiritual doorways of Hinduism and Buddhism where they not only believe in life for the soul after this one, but that the sum of a person's actions in the present incarnation is what determines the soul's fate in any future incarnations. Karma is the Hindu word for that fate—those inevitable circumstances that a soul is forced to endure in the afterlife as a result of everything it did or didn't do during the course of the current one. That's it. That's as radical as karma's definition gets. If it sounds kind of familiar, that's only because it's a theme found in just about every religion: accountability for the soul. While in this day and age we tend to use the word karma as an all-purpose metaphor for our universal punishment, our spiritual reward, or even our irreversible bad luck, it's original meaning has never been anything other than our own spiritual consequences for our own human actions. Of course, these consequences have a way of looking like vengeance, seeming like serendipity, and feeling like the wrath of god whenever they start swinging back our way at a time when we can't possibly deserve them, which is usually just a time when we're really not expecting them.

Think about that definition for a minute, and then ask yourself if any of those golden phrases you grew up with, such as "As you sow so shall you reap," "What goes around comes around," or "Do unto others as you would have them do unto you" are expressions that ring true for you, and if they are, well, then, you shouldn't have any problem with the laws of karma. At least not in theory, because in practice karma is simply the Universal Law of Compensation, otherwise known as the spiritual version of cause and effect. As most of you science enthusiasts would have to agree, it's not a whole lot different from the physical version. You know, Newton's third law of motion: "For every action there is an equal and opposite reaction." Coincidence? Not at all. That's the real purpose of this book—to get you to at least consider the theory that I believe our ancient astronomers not only embraced but implemented. Universal Law is based on scientific principles, and what's more, it begins in the heavens.

Enjoy the read, but if you want to get the most out of this book, please take my advice and read each chapter before flipping right to the placements that apply to you. Each individual chapter is my "one shot" at shifting your astrological perspective on that particular section of your birth chart, which means it's my one shot at throwing a little cold water on your soul. So take advantage of it. Your placement will end up having much more meaning on a much deeper level if I can get you to forget everything you've already learned about astrology, and force your soul to remember everything it conveniently forgot. Besides, I promise you won't get wet—hopefully, just a little wiser.

Before you go any further, you're going to need a copy of your own birth chart. Don't have one? Well then, just log on to any one of these websites below with the exact date, time, and city of your birth, and these cyber stargazers will not only calculate one for you in no time, they'll do it for you at no cost. Talk about good karma.

ASTROLABE
http://www.alabe.com/freechart/

Star 4Cast
http://www.star4cast.com/index2f.asp?page=home%2Easp

800 Horoscope
http://www.0800-horoscope.com/birthchart.php

1

The Birth Chart: Your Contract with the Universe

Young blood doth not obey an old decree:
We cannot cross the cause why we were born.

—WILLIAM SHAKESPEARE

So you want to know who you are and why you're here? Well, aside from rubbing a lamp, I suggest you take a look at your birth chart. Not the customary "Oh, with my 9th house Jupiter, I should have been a talk-show host" look, but perhaps a more spiritual look, one that requires a higher level of consciousness. As I'm sure most people would agree, within each one of us there's a distinct and vital life force that embodies the very essence of who we are and radiates our uniqueness to the outside world. We think of it as our "will" and call it our "soul" because it's been the core of our individuality for as long as we can remember, or as most people would argue, even longer. So would I, because, like most people, I believe that the soul is the eternal part of us—the spirit within that is constantly struggling to succeed as a human being in this world because it's really striving to evolve to a higher place in the spiritual one. According to my research, you probably do as well. Then why not study the birth chart from a perspective that allows us to observe the circumstances that shaped this inner spirit and created us? If we truly are in search of self-enlightenment, what view could reveal more of our human potential in this lifetime than one that is elevated enough to encompass the evolution of our soul before it got around to being us? With hindsight being what it is, an ounce of yesterday must surely be worth a pound of tomorrows, especially when a good look at yesterday not only reveals where our spiritual journey began once upon another lifetime, but also provides us with an invaluable glimpse of how much further we still have to go to live happily ever after in this one. Insightful stuff.

Fortunately for us, it's all right there, celestially reflected in the natal sky. We only have to find it, which is why we'd be smart to look at the birth chart as something more than just a computerized illustration of what was happening in the heavens on the day that we were born. While that's exactly what it is, when we view it from a spiritual perspective it becomes something even more: a celestial documentation of our soul's commitment to the universe, the one that explains why we came into the world and what we promised to do once we got here—what we like to call our purpose.

Is it any wonder that astrologers put so much importance on the birth chart? It shouldn't be. This pie-shaped diagram is more than just a picture of what the heavens looked like at the exact moment and from the precise location of a person's birth—it's actually two. From a physical perspective, it's a mathematical graph of the cosmic influences that were in effect at the precise moment a person took his or her first human breath. From a spiritual perspective, it's a personal record of that point in time when the soul showed up to report for duty in this lifetime. Confused? Ancient astronomers who practiced astrology and astronomy as one absolute science weren't. They embraced both perspectives and called it a horoscope (a universal view of the birth hour). Apparently they knew, even then, that environmental influences would always determine much of who we are, which is the reason this cryptic diagram was the primary tool of their trade.

To their way of thinking, we came into being by design, not by accident. They believed that the birth chart conclusively identified the specific energies that were previously chosen by the soul for this lifetime. They didn't refer to the horoscope as an astrological blueprint of an individual's cosmic chromosomes, but that's exactly how they used it. In fact, these early scientists determined the birth chart to be a celestial chart of real human potential because, as far as they were concerned, it was more than just a map of the influences that were in effect at birth. They believed it was a picture of the climate that actually created birth, a universal snapshot of our very earliest environment. No, not the environment that spawned those pivotal experiences of separation anxiety, sibling rivalry, or even mommy dearest, but the one that existed long before that—the first one. Think of it. A universal clock is ticking forward in time until, ultimately, it strikes the astronomical instant that's critical to the fundamental development of you. Critical because when that instant occurs it's the one that actually triggers the process of birth itself. Yours. Why? Because the moment the cosmos moved into the celestial energies that were previously chosen by your soul for this lifetime, the cosmic formula for you was activated. Is it any wonder then that you were born at that particular twinkling in time and space? How could it be? Obviously, it was your time. Literally, universally, and, of course, karmically.

So what does that mean? First of all, it means that your arrival on this planet was actually a spiritual appointment disguised as a physical event. Second of all, and even more amazing, the exact moment of your birth was never really an accident because it was always, technically, an agenda—your soul's agenda. Furthermore, because that agenda was reflected in the sky when you came into the world, astrologers call it a horoscope (a universal view of the birth hour). When that horoscope is put on paper in diagram form, it becomes what everyone calls your birth chart (a mathematical map of your birth energies for this lifetime). When that birth chart is being used to determine your soul's earthly progress and your spiritual evolution, it becomes something even more significant, something I call your contractual agreement with the universe—complete with timetables, incentives, and, if studied closely enough, even a little karmic fine print (which most astrologers just refer to as Neptune).

Now, let's be clear. This is not meant to suggest that in karmic astrology your horoscope is all about predestiny. It's not. While the soul's challenges in this lifetime are often karmic in nature, they are not about fate. That would imply that the cards have been dealt, the universe is in control, and the outcome is certain. With personal choice as part of this contract and, unfortunately, at your disposal, the universe, like the outcome, is subject to change without notice. Your horoscope is, however, about specific planetary positions that were provided at birth to outline the chosen boundaries of your own personal plan of development. These powerful energies simply function as your astrological compass, guiding you to certain experiences, situations, and relationships by generating the best circumstances to acknowledge and develop them.

This contract was purposely designed to provide the necessary opportunities for your personal growth and spiritual advancement. This means that although happiness and success are on the guest list, if disappointment and setback don't crash the party occasionally, there's no conflict. No insight. No growth. Comforting, isn't it, to know that the universe is on the job, and, apparently, at the door? Well, it should be, because while the soul is big on spiritual evolution, the ego is not and often rejects these unpleasant growth challenges for more immediate or rewarding opportunities, like fame, fortune, and, sadly, happy hour.

Ironically, whenever we give up a little growth for a lot of gratification, it just seems to propel us into the even less desirable throes of super heartache, mega failure, or jumbo loss. Divine punishment? Well, as much as that would give us great comfort and take us off the human hook, no. It's just a universal reminder that we really can't change old habits if we're just not doing anything to address them. Unfortunately, sometimes they are very old, and we ignore them even more. The cosmos, however, is undaunted and continuously gives each and every one of us chance after chance to address them until it is forced to resort to that angst-ridden whack across the egotistical head that always brings us to our emotional knees—the one that we never saw coming because we were so busy fighting those extraordinary obstacles and insurmountable difficulties that always seem to be almost purposely thrown into our willful paths just when we were too busy focusing on ourselves to notice. Where were the signs? After all, aren't we only human? Regrettably, yes, which is why our spiritual advancement tends to take us a while—often lifetimes. Evidently, the cosmos has the ability to knock us off the wrong track, but thanks to the ever-popular free will option in our contracts, not off our egos. Because of that, we continue to deny responsibility for anything that even resembles failure in our lives, preferring instead to exercise our universal birthright of assigning blame or just indulging in self-pity. After all, it's what allows us to continue that highly productive human pastime of jamming round pegs into square holes.

So much for universal guidance—but still, we'd be wise to remember that the universe, with all its infinite power, is not only unlimited in its ability to supply us with the opportunities for growth we have chosen, but is also surprisingly effective at surprising us whenever it does. This is what separates the wiser soul from the not-so-wiser soul; the ill-fated spirit that haplessly roams this planet from the more fortunate one that happily thrives on it. These scheduled growth opportunities are nothing less than our karmic forks in the road, and how we handle them determines our earthly fate as well as our spiritual destiny, because they are what force us to make those conscious human decisions that impact our unconscious immortal souls. These are the moments in our lives when we choose to either accept responsibility for the adversity in our lives or just sit back and curse the powers that be; to comply with the terms of our cosmic contract and evolve to the next level or, for those of us with hard hats and even harder heads, to just dig in our stubborn human heels and stay firmly put in self-serving nowhere—you know, our opportunities to improve our eternal lives or to just improve today's cash flow. Ultimately, we have choices, and, unfortunately, we tend to make them.

So then, wouldn't it make sense to find out where we tend to encounter these karmic crossroads in life? Or, more accurately, where you should start looking for them in your own life? You're about to find out, beginning at the top and starting with your own personal copy of your soul's contract with the universe: your birth chart.

Because you're always the star of your own horoscope (no matter what type of astrology you're practicing), the Sun is your personal marker and always represents you in one way or another in every type of birth chart. Thus, in karmic astrology (which is really just astrology for the soul), the Sun is your spiritual marker and represents you before you actually became you in this life. All forms of astrology, including spiritual astrology, recognize the inner natal planets like Mercury, Venus, Mars, and Jupiter as the personal planets that reflect your own chosen game plan for today. In karmic astrology the outer natal planets—in particular Saturn, Neptune, and Pluto—are actually your soul's planets. They represent the things that you did, or didn't do, yesterday—the things your soul promised to rectify and accomplish this time around.

Therefore, these outer planets are the ones that we focus on in this book. These are the energies that become your karmic crossroads in this life today because, long before you got here, they were your soul's lofty promises to the cosmos yesterday, the ones you should be keeping now. That is why studying the birth chart from this higher perspective makes keeping these promises a lot easier to do. After all, it provides the only earthly seat in the universal house where you can actually see them, and that's important because, when you can see them, your soul gets a conscious opportunity to remember them. That is not just a therapeutic experience for your soul, but an enlightening one for you as well, because it's how you finally get around to discovering that your natal Sun is more than just the somebody you could become today, it's the brilliant powerhouse you proved to be yesterday; or that your natal Saturn is not just an old karmic lesson waiting to be learned, it's a real grown-up ladder to success that's waiting to be climbed; that your natal Neptune doesn't just reflect your soul's unpaid emotional debt to the cosmos, it also reveals your best earthly method for paying it; that your natal Pluto is not just the overwhelming force that controlled you in the past, but it's also the promise you made to become more powerful in this lifetime because of it (hopefully without nuclear weapons). Finally, it's from this very exclusive astrological vantage point that you also get an opportunity to explore your soul's secret playground and favorite universal "junk drawer," the 12th house. This is where your soul likes to bury the unbearable past and everything it wants you to forget just so that you can wallow happily in denial by never remembering to deal with the pain. Even if you don't have any planets in this house, it's a powerful influence in your birth chart, so note the sign on the cusp, open your eyes, and buckle up—it's bound to be a bumpy ride.

The ride is worth it, because therapy usually is. As a universal map of your soul's personal plan of development you only have to study your horoscope from this slightly higher viewpoint and somewhat broader mindset to reveal a brand-new understanding of the most important person in your life: you. that's because there's really no better definition of enlightenment than coming to the realization that your so-called destiny is just a matter of showing up for the very experiences that you signed up for. Hard to believe? Of course it is. Who in their right mind would ever agree to the manipulative partnerships and destructive power struggles spawned by a Pluto in the 7th house? Or worse, volunteer to have the physical challenges and childhood inadequacies of Saturn in the first? No one. That's why the soul was left in charge of spiritual growth. It's also why the soul is, indeed, accountable for making sure that you get it in this life—but it's not just the soul. In fact, it's from this very elevated perspective that the cosmos has no choice but to hold you accountable as well. There are no universal passes on this one because, spiritually speaking, you actually signed on the dotted line yourself and physically acknowledged your very own horoscope as being your soul's one and only contractual agreement with the universe for this lifetime. How? You officially agreed to its terms and conditions with the one individual action that is as powerful as it is binding: your birth.

2

The Glyphs: Your Karmic Keys

Give me a key for this,
And instantly unlock my fortunes here.

—WILLIAM SHAKESPEARE

Before you start trying to make some cosmic sense out of your own horoscope, you may need some help finding your way around the birth chart. If not, feel free to skip this chapter completely. If you do, that's not a problem. Astrology may be a science, but it's not rocket science. This means that even though everyone's birth chart comes

Planet Glyphs	
Sun	☉
Saturn	♄
Neptune	♆
Pluto	♇

Sign Glyphs			
Aries	♈	Libra	♎
Taurus	♉	Scorpio	♏
Gemini	♊	Sagittarius	♐
Cancer	♋	Capricorn	♑
Leo	♌	Aquarius	♒
Virgo	♍	Pisces	♓

crammed to the midheaven with scary-looking symbols of planets and houses and signs, when it comes to getting a little karmic relief from your own chart, you only have to be on the lookout for the few I've listed above.

For the purposes of this book, you should know that you only have to locate four natal planets, look for twelve house numbers, and identify which one of the twelve constellations above are sitting on the cusp of your own 12th house. For the purposes of the glyph department, you also need to know that "natal planets" is a category that includes the Sun. Enlightenment doesn't get any easier than this, if you know where to look for it, so pull out your birth chart and let's get busy.

That begins by taking a minute to take a good look at your birth chart, because when you do, the first thing you'll see is that your chart, like every birth chart, is really just a diagram made up of three different circles in one. The first is an outer circle on the rim, the second is that larger circle with the spokes, and the third is that small hub-like circle nestled in the center of your chart. While most people think this three-ring configuration can be intimidating, it's important to know that, like everything else in the wonderful world of astrology, there's actually an impressive mathematical reason behind it. Like most mathematical reasons, however, it's one that tends to confuse everyone before it impresses anyone, so you're going to want the condensed version.

While everyone knows that astrologers need an accurate picture of the heavens at the moment of birth, what every astrologer knows is that there's really only one accurate way to get it. That's by applying the only three universal rulers that can measure it—the exact date, the exact time, and the exact place where the blessed event took place. That brings us back to that frequently asked question: "Why three circles?" In every birth chart these three circles are those three universal rulers. The outer circle on the rim is the one that reflects the exact date that your birth occurred, based on the mathematical position of the fixed stars in our constellations. The second, larger spoked circle in the middle is the one that represents the exact time of day that your birth occurred, based on the mathematical tilt of the earth's axis. The small, hub-like circle in the center is the one that represents the exact spot on this planet where your birth occurred, based on the mathematical coordinates of that location.

As amazing as that is, the impressive part is this: it's only by properly aligning these three circles to each other that astrologers are actually able to get the one thing they need to do their own thing—an unobstructed view of just what the sky looked like above, around, and below the very place where you took your first human breath, at the very moment you took it. In other words, a full 360° of the universal environment that created you—what they would call your natal sky.

Because a 360° natal sky is an awful lot of sky to keep track of, especially when a good 180° of it is always below the earth at any given moment, ancient astronomers knew that the planet-tracking process had to be made foolproof if they were going to keep the celestial mapmaking business fail-safe. After designating the left-hand side of the birth chart to represent all heavenly points east of the birthplace and the right-hand side to represent all heavenly points west of it, they then divided the entire sky around the birthplace into twelve different pie-shaped sections that they numbered and called "houses." Every house comes with that one dividing line or "cusp" that separates it from the house before it, which is why every birth chart comes with twelve spokes in the second circle. Because each one of these twelve houses represents a very specific 30° area of the sky above our planet, each one was permanently placed in numerical order, starting at the eastern horizon, around the only part of the birth chart that actually represents this planet—the small hub in the center that serves as the birthplace.

These twelve pie-shaped houses made out of everyone's natal sky are the twelve definitive neighborhoods of your very own solar system, and because of that, the only twelve places you could ever find anything that happened to be in it at the moment you were born. This not only makes planet-hunting in this glyph-ridden, three-ringed

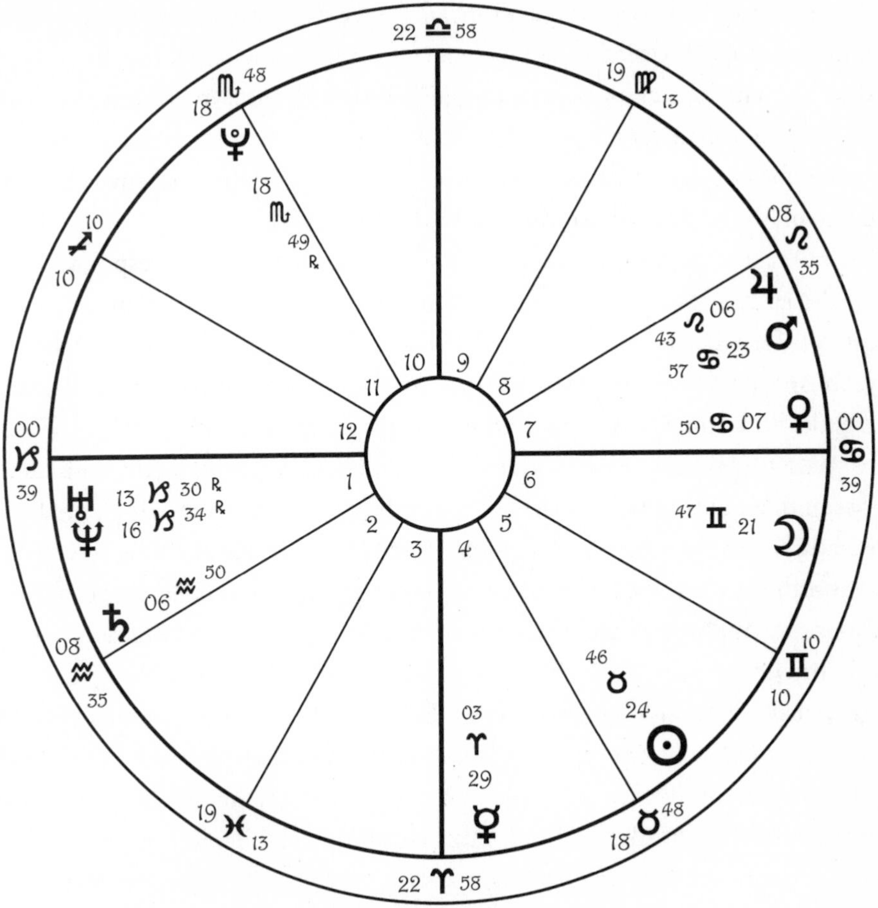

Ming-Koo Manning
May 15, 1991 / 11:00 PM / Chevy Chase, Maryland

circle much more scientific, it makes finding your own natal Sun, Saturn, Neptune, and Pluto a whole lot easier.

Here's a chart we can use as an example, the birth chart of my favorite four-legged gal pal, Ming-Koo, the family Shih Tzu. We'll locate and identify in Ming's chart whatever it is you'll be asked to locate and identify in your own chart later.

Based on the birth information displayed below her chart, Ming-Koo was born on May 15, 1991, in Chevy Chase, Maryland. That means the center hub is positioned to reflect the latitude and longitude of her birthplace. The constellations on the outer rim are aligned to reflect her May 15, 1991, birth date, and the large spoked circle in between is positioned to reflect the precise tilt of the earth at her 11:00 pm EDT birth time. With four natal planets on our list of things to locate, that's a good thing for us. With these three universal rulers on the job and doing the math, all we have to do is scan those twelve pie-shaped houses in the second circle of Ming's natal sky to see exactly where every planet was on the day she was born, at the time she was born, and from the place she was born, just as our own Sun, Saturn, Neptune, and Pluto will appear in our birth charts in the twelve sections that represent our very own solar system.

Now that we know where we should be looking, let's refer back to that list of planet glyphs in the beginning of this chapter to see what it is we should be looking for, beginning with the first and most important glyph on the list, the Sun. While we all know what it looks like in the sky, this is what you'll be looking for in the birth chart: ☉.

You've probably already spotted the Sun glyph sitting there on the bottom right-hand side of the chart. The pie-shaped section it's occupying is one of Ming-Koo's twelve natal houses. You'll find the small house number posted inside the narrow end of this pie-shaped section, close to the hub. As you can see, 5 is the house number of Ming's Sun, which means 5 is also the neighborhood number of the particular section of the sky that the Sun was occupying when Ming came into the world.

Locating a natal planet involves more than just determining which section of the natal sky it was occupying at the moment of birth. It also entails identifying which constellation it was moving through as well. Even though most of us know that anyone born on May 15 of any year was actually born during the Sun's yearly journey through the constellation of Taurus, Ming doesn't, so let's pretend that you don't either. After you've located the house position of the Sun's glyph in the birth chart, find the constellation glyph that's directly in line with and closest to the Sun's glyph inside the same house. (Pay no attention to the numbers, just concentrate on the glyphs.) The small constellation glyph that lines up closest to Ming's Sun glyph there inside house number 5 is ♉, the constellation glyph for Taurus, the Bull, giving Ming a Taurus Sun sign. In less time than it takes to read this chapter, you learned that Ming-Koo was born with a Taurus Sun in the 5th house by reading her birth chart.

It's Saturn's turn to be found, so you'll be looking for this: ♄.

The pie-shaped house that Saturn's glyph is occupying is number 1, and the constellation glyph that's closest to Saturn's glyph inside house number 1 looks like this: ♒—Aquarius.

Next is Neptune: ♆, also in the 1st house **in the sign of Capricorn:** ♑.

Pluto is the last planet to locate: ♇, in the 11th house in the sign of Scorpio: ♏.

All four natal planets are present and accounted for. It gets easier with each planet, because every natal planet is always located in the very same way in everyone's birth chart, including your own. To locate your natal planets, just follow the same four steps you followed to find Ming's: determine which glyph identifies the planet, which pie-shaped house the planet glyph is occupying, which 1 through 12 number is posted near the hub of that pie-shaped house, and which one of the twelve constellation glyphs is closest to that planet and inside the same house. It's simply that simple.

With that, it's time to advance to our final category here in chapter 2: cusps. The twelve spoke-like dividing lines in the birth chart are called cusps. These lines not only separate the natal houses from each other, but also serve as the twelve official doorways into each house. Even though every house in the birth chart has two dividing lines for sides, every house has only one cusp, the one dividing line that separates it from the house before it numerically. That means everything, because it means that everyone's 12th house cusp is always the one line in the birth chart that divides their 12th house from their 11th house, the only line that serves as a doorway into their 12th house. Therefore, to find Ming's 12th house cusp, you need to scan all those pie-shaped sections in her chart until you find the one with the small number 12 near the hub, up there on the left-hand side of the chart. The dividing line in that house that separates it from her 11th house, in the 10 o'clock position, is the astrological doorway into Ming's 12th house: her 12th house cusp. You can determine which constellation was positioned in that 12th house doorway at the moment she was born by following that 12th house cusp line up to the top of the house until the line hits the outer rim of the birth chart. Remember, this outer circle on the rim of the chart is the one that measures the position of the constellations at birth. Inside the rim and just above the point where the 12th house cusp line ends is this constellation glyph. This glyph, ♐, means Sagittarius was the constellation on Ming-Koo's 12th house cusp on May 15, 1991, at 11:00 pm EDT.

As easy as this was, it will be even easier when you're house hunting in your own chart. That's because while there aren't too many absolute or really sure things about the 12th house, the one absolute thing about it is that, like every other house, it's always in the same place in everyone's birth chart. So is its cusp.

Now that you've successfully located all the required planets, rogue constellations, and ambiguous cusps in Ming-Koo's birth chart, you're ready to start doing it all over again in a more important chart: your own. If somewhere along the way, however, you find yourself looking for glyphs in all the wrong places or not finding cusps in any of the right ones, it may help to come back to Chapter 2, even if it's just to be reminded that sometimes in the wonderful world of astrology, some things are always in the same place.

3

The Sun Sign: Your Karmic Degree

Not all the water in the rough rude sea
Can wash the balm from an anointed king.

—WILLIAM SHAKESPEARE

When it comes to karmic astrology, it's always best to start in the beginning—the cosmic beginning. According to cosmic legend, sometime after the much-celebrated big bang, our souls were dispatched to this planet to succeed as human beings in order to master materiality and advance in the spiritual world. According to cosmic law, however, the only way the soul could complete this lofty assignment was by making an honorable human mark on the physical world. While this may sound like something our wise old souls could do easily, it's important to keep in mind that an honorable human mark is not just honorable—it's also human. There was the dilemma. If our spiritual advancement in the hereafter was completely dependent on our physical achievement in the here and now, our selfless souls were going to have to step up and virtually hit one out of the park down here on planet Earth. A spiritual home run in the material world was not going to happen if our souls were allowed to aimlessly wander onto the field of human life whenever the weather suited them. This meant that body and soul were going to have to come together as one in this incarnation—as us. Together, we were going to have to keep that promise and make that honorable mark by creating something the body had worked for and the soul could be proud of—an honorable human life. That brings us to the single most significant factor in the solar system and the most important clause in your contract with the universe: the Sun.

As the earth's central source of heat and light, the Sun is a brilliant star that burns ninety-three million miles away in the middle of our solar system. Once a year it makes a path through twelve different constellations on an imaginary celestial beltway we call the ecliptic. As an influence in the heavens, this star dominates our existence, empowers our world, and gives us life. As an influence in the horoscope, it's what differentiates you from everyone else, energizes your ego, and spawns your personality. From an astrological perspective, it's who you are. Therefore, from a spiritual perspective, it's your karmic marker, or, as most karmic astrologers see it, your soul's personal promise to the universe that you, in this lifetime, will make a powerful effort to make something of yourself. That means rising to a position of authority, blinding the world with your brilliance, and empowering those around you. No pressure—just your soul's personal pledge to go out there and literally hit one out of the park. Sounds easy? If you think, as most people do, that this means nothing more than just living up to the general description of your Sun sign, you're right, that is too easy.

The fact of the solar matter is, no effort or conscious thought is even necessary for *being* our Sun sign, which is why we never put any into it. Those energies are second nature to each one of us. In fact, while most of us believe that we actually do personify the characteristics of our Sun's astrological sign, many of us think it's because we automatically absorbed the energies of the solar environment we just happened to be born into. The truth is we should think again—we should think higher.

Perhaps from the vantage point of the soul's perspective, it's no coincidence that each one of those twelve constellations on the ecliptic represents a different, yet significant, level of man's earthly evolution. That's because from a spiritual perspective, these are actually the twelve universal courses that are not only available to our souls for their development, but must be mastered by us for their advancement. While some souls are more ambitious than others and advance quicker, the karmic buzz is that every single one of our souls will master every single one of these levels—eventually, individually, and physically. That is tough for both body and soul because that means we must master these courses as animalistic human beings here on the unforgiving landscape of materialistic planet Earth. As if that wasn't enough entertainment for the cosmos, we're expected to learn them in no particular order and, apparently, in no definitive time frame, just until we get it right, which is why some courses are likely to take a lifetime to master. Others are even more likely to take twenty. As expected, there'll be lots of earthly mayhem, over many human lifetimes. Fortunately, if there's one thing the universe has plenty of, it's time, which means if there's one thing we should expect to do plenty of, it's lifetimes.

That leads us to ask "why?" After all, what good is the experience of previous lives spent wandering through the obstacle-strewn minefields of different constellations if we can't remember them? Especially when they seem to have no bearing on this life. In fact, our soul does remember them, even if we don't, and by studying the Sun's placement from a spiritual perspective, the soul's perspective, we get to see that these previous lifetimes do, indeed, have a bearing on this life. Furthermore, we get to see how knowing that in this life could actually change it. For starters, we get to see the real reason why we were born during the Sun's journey through a specific astrological sign, which ends up being a better, more enlightening one than we knew—a more simple one.

We were born when the Sun was occupying a particular astrological sign because that constellation is actually our soul's most previous level of spiritual growth, and because of that, it reflects our own current level of earthly expertise. This constellation, our Sun sign, not only reveals the cosmic course we satisfactorily completed under the universe's watchful eye in our last lifetime, but it also identifies how we are now karmically qualified to be a shining example of authority, power, and creativity just because we did complete the course. No wonder we can't help but project the qualities of this astrological sign without thinking. No wonder its energies are second nature to us. On some deep level, we've already worked, learned, and mastered everything it represents. This means that on some even deeper level, our Sun sign is our universal education—our soul's spiritual credentials and our karmic degree. Like the knowledge and skills that come with any degree that's been earned, the energies of this sign have been ingrained in our soul so they're ours to keep, but mostly to use. While we have all learned to trust those flashes of brilliant insight and unexplained know-how that always seem to come to us through the characteristics of our Sun sign, we'd really be much wiser and a lot happier if we learned to recognize them for what they really are—a universal roll call.

Those moments of unexpected savvy are supposed to remind us that we not only have a universal education, we also have a spiritual agenda to use it—hence, our karmic degree. For instance, you weren't brought into the world with a remarkable talent for the discovery and exchange of language, information, people, and ideas just because you were lucky enough to be born with a Gemini Sun. It's actually the other way around. You were purposely brought into the world when the Sun was wending its way through the Gemini constellation because you have a previously earned degree in communications and networking, and the universe is now waiting for you to pick it up and start using it. Of course, the universe has probably been waiting a few lifetimes for most of you Geminis, but being occasionally undependable and frequently superficial is how you were taught to keep the world more interesting, and us more interested in it.

If, on the other hand, you were born at a time when the Sun was occupying Pisces, you can be sure that in one of your less-hazy previous lifetimes you aced the course in dissolving boundaries and softening the harsh concepts of reality. You're a real pain magnet in this life, but that's only because you're now a bona fide rehabilitation expert who's desperately seeking a victim, and until one can be found, you're only too willing to volunteer for the position yourself.

With a Scorpio Sun, there's no question about it—you're a professional survivor with a previously earned master's degree in emotional intimacy, unknown forces, and life and death issues. You're nothing less than a real card-carrying defense expert who, if the truth be told, is secretly empowered by your own deep desires and even more empowered by the deeper resources that just don't belong to you, and never will.

Is your Sun in Virgo? Then, so is your karmic degree, which is why you're unequaled in the analyses and repair of data, policy, procedures, and people. You're the highly credentialed, though never appointed, problem-solving critic who somewhere along the imperfect path to perfection somehow developed an annoying addiction to fact-finding and micromanaging. You're the one who is always quick to point out the flaws, but that's only because you're the one who was universally trained to find them.

What about you with your Sun in Libra? As someone who was celestially schooled in the fine art of keeping it fair, keeping it together, and keeping the peace, you're a behind-the-scenes strategist who has no trouble seeing all sides of any situation and even less trouble spotting every wolf in sheep's clothing, a professional partner who, somewhere in the diplomatic past, majored in manipulation and minored in peace-at-all-costs.

How about that Sagittarius Sun of yours? For starters, no one is more qualified to heroically pursue and masterfully promote any kind of truth, knowledge, justice, and adventure. Of course, no one is more likely to self-righteously dismiss our beliefs and opinions while doing so either. You're the one who was universally trained to live by your heart and die for your beliefs, which explains why you never seem to have any difficulty sharing them with us, and why you always seem to have even less difficulty changing them after you do. Can you see where this is going? You didn't just inherit your Sun sign—you learned it, and the universe is waiting for you to use it.

Therefore, you must use that Sun sign—in this life and at this time—because when all is astrologically said and done, your natal Sun sign is the education, wisdom, and expertise that was earned by your soul for that very purpose—your purpose, which is why this sign can't help but radiate the essence of your uniqueness. It's what personifies the core of your potential, not just by reflecting who you are and where you've been, but by radiating what you've learned and how far you can go. This is your karmic degree, and, like any other degree, it validates your creative excellence to the world by reminding you, as well as everyone who crosses your path, of the brilliant and honorable solar energies that are available to you throughout this lifetime. These are the very same energies that you're going to need to make something of yourself, and your mark on the world. In fact, it's for that very reason that the constellation the Sun was traveling through at your birth, your Sun sign, is your universal access to power and the first compelling half of the solar clause in your cosmic contract—the part where you not only promised the cosmos that you would play to win in this life, but that you would do it by using the previously mastered energies of this astrological sign to shine, dazzle, lead, and dominate your way to the big leagues. Don't look now, but it's game time.

Sun in Aries

I have immortal longings in me.

—WILLIAM SHAKESPEARE

Karmic Degree: Ego, Independence, and the Physical Self.
Aries is ruled by Mars, the planet of ego and physical action.

As someone who began life while the Sun was moving through Aries, your previous path of soul development was one of personal independence through the lessons of the physical self. This means that you are now here in this lifetime to show the rest of us how to lead and inspire through those ego-building experiences of personal ambition, independent accomplishment, and physical involvement. In short, you're supposed to be annoyingly self-directed. You're the one who has successfully mastered the ambitious assignment of becoming an independent individual—primarily by not being afraid to be one. This brings us to why this spiritual agenda may sound a little too good to be true. It's all about you—but hey, it's supposed to be. That's because, astrologically speaking, the Sun shines strong when it's placed in the esteem-drenched energies of the Aries constellation, which explains why this solar degree comes equipped with an incredible ego that demands nothing less than complete personal freedom. Apparently, you have to be aware of the world from only your own point of view because, ultimately, you have to be able to do what you were trained to do—act in the moment. The universe expects you to be out there blazing new trails, living on the edge, and leaping before you look. Obviously, that's not the agenda of ordinary mortals, but you'd be the first to agree—you're not even close to falling into that category. In fact, this Aries diploma was actually earned by learning how to courageously pursue and confidently confront danger, conflict, challenge, and opposition.

Evidently, when it comes to decisive, immediate action, you're truly without peer. However, as the highly competitive, determined-to-win master of uncharted territory, you're also without cold feet. Universal resumes just don't get more impressive than this, but then, neither do the challenges. This is really not a problem for someone who's majored in immortality, someone who's managed to earn their cosmic credentials by consistently playing to win, undauntedly seizing the day and courageously getting there first—someone like you. No wonder you're celestially certified to be our shining example of individual achievement and personal excellence. You're the one who is karmically qualified to conquer the world. Unfortunately, however, you're also officially obligated to do it without demanding to be the center of our universe. As difficult as it is to believe, when it comes right down to it, you're not obligated. Although you've been blessed with a remarkable ego that is capable of accomplishing just about anything, it carries a planetary prerequisite that stipulates you are never to let yourself be controlled by its dominant energy in any way. Instead, you must achieve your physical success and realize your personal greatness with independent actions that are confident and assertive, not selfish and inconsiderate. Yes, there is a difference, and no, there are no exceptions. Apparently, immortality may take a while.

Not surprisingly, at your brightest, no one is more spontaneous, motivated, pioneering, and courageous. You always set out to accomplish the impossible, and, one way or another, you usually manage to succeed. Most importantly, you are passionately fearless as you energize us with your strong sense of self and your enthusiasm for life. Rarely overwhelmed, we marvel at your willingness to not only accept but also to initiate those projects that everyone else seems to decline or avoid. Unfortunately, because your powerful ego often exceeds your actual ability, you're just as likely to leave them unfinished when they become too detailed or boring. Then, when praise isn't forthcoming and success isn't immediate, we watch as you impatiently trample on anyone in your path, arrogantly blame the incompetence of others, or just selfishly shortcut your narcissistic way to your own self-serving objective. You become headstrong, pushy, childish, and confrontational as your inability to see anything other than your own perspective ignites your hot temper and inflames your reckless impatience. At these very dark moments, you're at your egotistical, bullying, and tyrannical worst.

We shouldn't be surprised. After all, you're the universal warrior who has never failed to amaze us with not only your willingness to stand up and be counted, but with your ability to surpass even your own expectations when doing so. It's your purpose. Besides, that remarkable ego of yours just wouldn't have it any other way, which is why you always seem to have more spirited confidence and passionate courage than is humanly possible, and why the mere presence of your company seems to encourage our independence and inspire us on to our own even loftier goals. But then, with a degree in Aries, the universe has chosen you to demonstrate what real leadership looks like. Why else would you always be fearlessly leading the battle, intentionally rushing into harm's way, or heroically defying the odds? Obviously, it's your karmic responsibility, and, apparently, you're not surprised. Unlike us, you know you've been endowed with an extraordinary ego that provides you with tremendous willpower and an insatiable appetite for accomplishment. You know that you're expected to use this fearless sense of self to inspire others to take risks and achieve their best. On some level, you're even aware that by doing so, you're unequivocally equipped with an exclusive passport to the very noble destination of being first among equals and foremost in honor. This just happens to be your very own cosmic catch-22. What you may not know is this: despite your soul's immortal success in a previous life and your own earthly guarantees for experiencing it again in this one, that independent ego of yours is quite likely to have other plans.

Cosmic Theme Song: "I Am, I Said" by Neil Diamond

Sun in Taurus

He that wants for money, means and content
is without three good friends.

—WILLIAM SHAKESPEARE

Karmic Degree: Personal Values, Material Resources, and Results.
Taurus is ruled by Venus, the planet of love, beauty, and pleasure.

As someone who began life while the Sun was moving through Taurus, your previous path of soul development was one of physical growth through the lessons of personal values. This means that you are now here in this lifetime to show the rest of us how to produce and appreciate the tangible benefits of physical comfort, material possessions, and concrete results. Obviously, this is one spiritual agenda that won't be hard to live up to because, happily, it demands nothing less than contentedly living the good life, which, for the most part, requires nothing more than putting your own physical gratification at the top of your spiritual "to do" list. Now before those visions of hard cash and soft furniture start dancing in your head, you should be advised that no one gets a universal pass, not even when your spiritual agenda comes with a gold card. Apparently, yours does because when you've brilliantly completed the karmic requirements of a Taurus degree, you've expertly mastered all the skills necessary to physically acquire and reliably maintain value, stability, satisfaction, and results. Yes, apparently your compulsion to obsessively hoard all that financial security and passionately lust after material reward is much more than just your reason for getting up in the morning. It's your karmic responsibility.

You're the cosmic connoisseur who is here for no other purpose than to personify the universal meaning of earthly prosperity, which requires nothing more than just being a shining example of what you have already learned how to do—thrive. No wonder you never seem to have any difficulty possessing whatever it is you appreciate, and, as most of us can attest to, every difficulty parting with it after you do. You've been celestially schooled in the fine art of holding on to value, which is why you were born with an incredible eye for beauty and a remarkable sense of quality. It's also why the finer things in life can actually be the primary source of your misery when, for one reason or another, you just can't get your hands on them—or, worse, we can.

According to the cosmos, in order to be able to possess value, you must first be able to define it, which means that before you can stake your claim in the material world, you must first develop a reliable value system. You know, a personal set of guiding principles that forces you to strive for the excellence that you're here to personify without stubbornly resisting the change that is needed for growth—personal growth—the kind that makes you a better human being, not just a richer one. A possible fly in the cosmic ointment? Possibly, because although your Taurus degree certifies that no one is more qualified to recognize the net worth of reliability or appreciate the real value of consistency, the universe won't let you grow materially if you refuse to grow personally. That means that before you can possess anything of value, build anything permanent, or keep anything worth having, you must first relinquish the notion that change, like an empty stomach or an uncomfortable chair, is something to be avoided at all costs. Or, unfortunately, it will cost you.

Understandably, on your best days, you can be practical, deliberate, strong, and capable. Most importantly, you're dependable. You inspire those around you with your stamina for hard work and your determination to finish the projects that others have long since abandoned. When the going gets tough, you always manage to impressively keep your head, unfailingly keep your promises, and relentlessly keep us going. Yes, no one is more remarkable, but then, no one is more reliable. Unfortunately, however, your best asset is also your worst liability and very much the unreasonable reason for your less-appealing days. You know, those dark days when that steadfast perseverance of yours is reduced to stubborn inflexibility just because your personal values were challenged or your physical security was threatened—or you thought they were. That is when you start to become the most imposing hardhead, intimidator, and miser we will ever experience, and we get to watch you angrily conserve all your personal resources, possessively cling to whatever you regard as your own, and selfishly take great pains to accumulate wealth that you never intend to use or share.

What options do you have? As the universal ambassador to our worldly existence, you must now be the personification of reliable physical results. You're the one who is supposed to reap the benefits of the material world because you're the one who is here to demonstrate its most important principle: "What we choose to own is simply a material reflection of what we deem worthwhile." That is why you're now expected to share your cosmic wisdom with us. No wonder you've been endowed with all that is necessary to achieve your material goals and satisfy your physical appetites. The world is watching your every materialistic move. Through your spiritual example, we're supposed to learn that on this earthly plain only strength will move mountains and value is always compensated. Through your personal example, we must be made to realize that material ownership is never without physical responsibility. Which means that although your first territorial trick is showing us how to hold on to our belongings without nailing them down, that's not the hard part of living up to your karmic credentials. With a degree in Taurus, your biggest celestial challenge lies in your ability to show us that real value has nothing to do with price. Okay, so some mountains are bigger than others.

Cosmic Theme Song: "You Can't Always Get What You Want" by the Rolling Stones

Sun in Gemini

I have bought golden opinions from all sorts of people.

—WILLIAM SHAKESPEARE

Karmic Degree: Communication, Education, and Networking.
Gemini is ruled by Mercury, the planet of the mind and intellect.

As someone who began life while the Sun was moving through Gemini, your previous path of soul progression was one of intellectual development through the experience of the immediate environment. This means that you are now here in this lifetime to connect the rest of us to each other through those stimulating channels of communication, education, commerce, and transportation. Obviously, this is the global grapevine of spiritual agendas because, apparently, you are the one who was born to investigate, circulate, articulate, and, yes, aggravate the complex circuitry of our ordinary lives. This is why you can't help but explore every exciting option as you navigate every existing network just to find every conflicting opinion, and, of course, challenge everyone else's thinking. You're the cosmic conduit who is here to engage our minds in the outside world by stimulating our curiosity in the collective neighborhood. While that's really nothing more than just somehow getting us to focus our misguided attention on whatever happens to be holding yours, one thing's for certain, nobody does it better. The other thing that's for certain is nobody knows how, because this Gemini degree was officially earned by brilliantly mastering the only cosmic course available in the discovery and exchange of language, information, people, and ideas.

It's no wonder your keen powers of observation keep you so incredibly aware of your own surroundings and so remarkably adaptable to ours. You've been universally trained to instantly process and deftly deliver just about anything that crosses your path, or, when that gets too boring, your mind. To our amazement, nothing ever escapes your attention. To yours, nothing ever satisfies it, but that's only because you really can't be stimulating to us if the world isn't interesting to you. In fact, you're constantly compelled to bounce from one exciting escapade to another and from each provocative person to the next simply because it's now your karmic responsibility to keep us intellectually involved and reliably informed with the fascinating feedback of your exhilarating experiences.

That brings us to your ongoing obsession with diversity and your never-ending battle with boredom—otherwise known as the cosmic twin hurdles that keep you from being as interesting as you could be and as knowledgeable as you should be because they keep you constantly skimming the superficial surface of everyone and everything. That's a bit of a problem for you because, although this Gemini degree certifies that no one is better equipped to be a shining example of brilliant communications, it also stipulates that you are the one who must do so responsibly, or lose your credibility. Evidently, you're only kept firmly in our loop by keeping us reliably in the know. That requires not only skillfully probing that impenetrable surface and cleverly finding those difficult answers, but doing it brilliantly without carelessly tapping those questionable sources or dangerously draining the depths of our patience.

You see, according to your karmic qualifications and unlike the local pizzeria, the universe is expecting a lot more from you in this lifetime than just variety and speed.

Understandably then, you can be articulate, clever, informative, and humorous. Most importantly, you have the astrological advantage of an extremely agile mind and a highly developed learning capacity. This is often mistaken for just plain old smoke and mirrors as this combination not only manifests as an impressive ability to think on your feet, but an amazing facility for pulling the occasional rabbit out of your eleventh-hour hat from other positions as well. In fact, this adaptable intellect is the real reason you happen to have two distinct and often opposing sides to your personality. In a previous life you learned that the best way to become more effective in your environment was to become more versatile in your thinking. Therefore, at a very early age in this one, you discovered that by simply concealing that part of your persona that didn't get the attention or approval you needed you could make your somewhat hostile environment a lot more user-friendly. Consequently, the other you was born. That's right, you really do have a twin self, which explains why you have the ability to display more cleverness and dexterity than is humanly possible on most days and why you often seem to possess the curiosity, impatience, and inconsistency of someone with a multiple personality disorder on all of the others. That's a theory we tend to consider whenever you start randomly jumping to erroneous conclusions or spontaneously neglecting the relevant facts while recklessly dismissing the significant consequences. You know, on your dark days when your creative commentary and childish discontent never fail to demonstrate just how intrusive, deceptive, and shallow you really can be.

It's not surprising. With a degree in Gemini, one way or another you must get our attention, because sooner or later, you must stimulate our thinking. You're dedicated to working us into the web of your mental community because you're committed to the development of our mental awareness. Apparently, the universe has endowed you with enough flexibility of thought and action to keep every one of us entertained by the both of you for quite some time. As the communicating link in our planetary network, you have both the power to open our minds and the potential to close our eyes. That means that you can connect us to each other with exciting information or divide us from each other with lies and misconceptions. Your difficulties only seem to occur when either one of you is unable to tell the difference between the two.

Cosmic Theme Song: "Keep the Customer Satisfied" by Simon & Garfunkel

Sun in Cancer

It is the very error of the Moon;
She comes more near the earth than she was want,
and makes men mad.

—WILLIAM SHAKESPEARE

Karmic Degree: Emotional Security and Domestic Stability.
Cancer is ruled by the Moon, the celestial guardian of human emotions.

As someone who began life while the Sun was moving through Cancer, your previous path of soul development was one of emotional nourishment through the lessons of domestic security. This means that you are now here in this lifetime to show the rest of us how to cherish and preserve the emotional sanctuaries of home, family, maternal care, and the ancestral past. By universal design, you have no choice but to absorb anything you feel, and reflect everything you sense, simply because you are the one who was universally trained to respond to the primal needs of the world around you. This is why you're so acutely sensitive to even the most subtle impressions in your immediate environment, as well as the most hard-to-read people in ours. You were born to be our emotional mirror. That explains a lot, doesn't it? In fact, you earned this Cancer degree by learning how to instinctively create and skillfully sustain the support, belonging, protection, and intimacy that is not only critical to domestic stability, but essential to emotional survival.

The good news is, your instincts are as remarkable as they are reliable. In fact, they compel you to collect everything and encourage you to discard nothing because it is now your universal purpose to provide enough of whatever is needed to make everyone feel safe and nurtured. Can you imagine—an astrological degree that not only endorses your ability to use love, money, and food as your very own emotional pacifiers, but provides you with a planetary permit for hoarding them as well. Obviously, this is the pay dirt of spiritual agendas—your once-in-a-blue-moon cosmic calling—but not so fast. While your Cancer degree does confirm that no one else is more karmically qualified to be a shining example of compassionate caretaking, and that you alone are the one who was trained to create a sense of belonging for those who need it, it also stipulates that, at least in this particular lifetime, you must do so without ignoring emotional boundaries. That's right—the bad news, and you may need to get your therapist on the phone for this one—the cosmos is expecting you to make others feel nurtured and secure in this lifetime without draining yourself in the process, or worse, smothering us in the aftermath.

As daunting as that sounds, apparently there's more. Even though your amazing ability to preserve our familiar habits and protect the nostalgic past are two of your most hard-earned Cancer skills, you're not allowed to use them as your own cosmic loopholes for obsessively clinging to useless objects, old resentments, or obsolete behaviors. Evidently, before you can provide the emotional sustenance we need, you must first show us how to let go of the things that we don't, and you must do it by example. No, this is not universal torture, and yes, a blue moon is a lot more likely.

Understandably, then, on your bright days, you are compassionate, creative, industrious, and loyal. Most importantly, you're a creature of instinct who is amazingly tenacious and has no trouble reaching your goals. In fact, with a propensity for indirect routes, a belief in gut feelings, and a knack for keeping under the radar, your ambitions are often surprisingly underestimated, even by those who know you best. They shouldn't be. You're the self-designated guardian who can always achieve even the most difficult objective because you can't ever resist surrounding the people and projects you love with genuine concern and excellent care. Unfortunately, however, in your eagerness to supply whatever you feel is needed at the time, you have been known to become intolerably smothering and unbearably possessive.

In fact, there's really no one better at hanging on to the things, people, and feelings that have managed to outlive both their usefulness and our patience than you. On these dreary days, you can be either demanding, needy, fearful, or suffocating—sometimes even all of the above—which is when, invariably, as a voluntary prisoner of your own self-absorbed emotions, you become quite variable. We then stand by and watch in disbelief as you wax obsessive and wane neurotic, reliving all of the numerous, if not imagined, slights, rejections, and humiliations that, for one unthinkable reason or another, you've been forced to endure. At a time like this, what else can you do but wallow in self-pity and be so conspicuously miserable? Not much. After all, with a degree in Cancer, one way or another, someone is going to be nurtured. It's your purpose, but then it was once your major. That is why you will always instinctively provide whatever it takes to support, protect, and defend the welfare of anyone you feel happens to need it. Unlike us, you have both a superior ability to be intimate and a remarkable talent for preservation. Although we're continuously amazed by your capacity to respond to others in a way that is never less than clairvoyant, we're even more impressed, and somewhat envious, that you're never less than extremely comfortable doing so. Ironically, you may be a little too comfortable. Because you've been instilled with such profound insight and infused with such instinctual empathy, you will always have great difficulty ignoring anyone who needs support, cries out for attention, or longs for understanding. While that's exactly how you were trained to fulfill your universal purpose and realize your solar potential, you'll never be able to achieve your personal greatness unless you can first get past the most compelling bleeding heart in your immediate environment: you.

Cosmic Theme Song: "Shame On the Moon" by Bob Seger

Sun in Leo

How like a winter hath my absence been.

—WILLIAM SHAKESPEARE

Karmic Degree: Personal Distinction and Creative Brilliance. As the celestial guardian of the human ego, the Sun rules the sign of Leo.

As someone who began life while the Sun was moving through Leo, your previous path of soul development was one of personal distinction through the expression of the creative self. This means that you are now here in this lifetime to show the rest of us how to skillfully generate and honorably glorify those basic internal powers of spirited vitality, courageous leadership, and creative brilliance. Apparently, you have no choice but to invigorate the masses and brighten the world. You are the powerful life source who is here to supply us with the energy that we desperately need in order to have confidence in ourselves. In fact, your Leo degree was actually earned by learning how to expertly radiate and confidently celebrate life, power, love, and talent. No wonder you never have any difficulty taking center stage, impressing the little people, and grabbing the applause. Like the Sun, your universal purpose is to enhance life on this planet by dazzling everyone on it with your amazing ability to do what you do best: shine. While it may be difficult for us to believe, your determination to be the center of our universe is actually more than just an egotistical whim—it's your karmic responsibility. Remarkably, your devotion to this duty has no limitations, conditions, or even strings attached. Unfortunately, your ego does, which is why your supremacy really must be acknowledged and your performance had better be appreciated if all is to remain right with the world.

Obviously, this is a very small price for us to pay as we willingly move around you, content to spend our lives circling your splendor for the very confidence, charisma, and courage that we ourselves lack. Now, as far as spiritual agendas go, it really doesn't get much better than being issued one that comes with a crown. However, at the risk of bursting a royal bubble or two, the universe insists that even you have a cosmic criterion to live up to. This, of course, would be that privilege always has responsibility. This means that although your Leo degree certifies that you are now karmically qualified to be a shining example of the powerful forces of life, it also stipulates that you must always do so with the honorable intention of inspiring everyone to access their own creative energies, not for the far-less-noble purpose of encouraging anyone to depend on yours. Evidently, the cosmos is expecting you to use your talent, authority, and leadership to empower those around you, not enslave them to you. While enforcing this celestial stipulation may require an intervention of sorts, that's only because waking up to an adoring public every day is not just a birthright you've come to enjoy, it's an addiction you're loathe to relinquish.

Understandably then, at your brightest, you can be strong, generous, affectionate, and loyal. Your passion for drama and your appetite for authority keeps you happily in the spotlight and heroically in charge. Most importantly, we can count on you—not just because you always do whatever you must to earn your way into that responsible position of leadership, but because you always do whatever it takes to justify the confidence that's been placed in you once you get there. In fact, your inherent ability to always stay the course when everyone else around you has lost both the patience and stamina to go the distance is usually when we get our first glimpse of your incredible determination, heartfelt loyalty, and unwavering sense of duty. Yes, much to our amazement, you really are extraordinary. Much to your amazement, we took far too long to notice, and while that's probably true, it's usually because even though your fixity of purpose is something we greatly admire, it's actually brought to us by the very same dominant will and king-sized ego that we don't admire. You know, the one that compels you to use your incredible willpower as nothing more than a fierce resistance to any kind of change that is not of your own making, which also serves the even more egotistical purpose of keeping you from ever admitting the many mistakes that are. This is otherwise known as plain old stubborn pride, and otherwise experienced as the astrological Achilles' heel that eventually causes you to crash and burn because it inevitably compels you to cling to all those bad relationships, poor ideas, and, of course, your own inflexible way. While that's one path that isn't always paved with selfless intentions, it's often the most surprisingly direct route to the biggest dictator, bully, or show-off we never knew existed—the one you become in your dark moments, when you're at your arrogant, demanding, outrageous, and self-centered worst.

With a degree in Leo, what did we expect? As the infinite life force who was universally trained to leave your personal mark on our dark and dreary world, you will not be ignored. You were born to assume a position of leadership because you were taught to believe in your own power. In fact, from where we commoners sit, you've obviously been endowed with all that is necessary to reign supreme, including the unwavering conviction that eventually you will. That, apparently, is what validates your sovereignty and certifies your greatness. Your only real challenge lies in your ability to demonstrate the universal principle that respect, like applause, must be earned, by using your powerful influence and creative brilliance to make everyone's life more productive and meaningful—not just your own more powerful—to serve the little people's needs, not just your ego. You must shine with confident authority, but only because you've been universally trained to inspire ours.

Cosmic Theme Song: "Here Comes the Sun" by the Beatles

Sun in Virgo

Find out the cause of this effect,
Or rather say, the cause of this defect,
For this effect defective comes by cause.

—WILLIAM SHAKESPEARE

Karmic Degree: Physical Perfection and Practical Service.
Virgo is ruled by Mercury, the planet of the mind and intellect.

As someone who began life while the Sun was moving through Virgo, your previous path of soul development was one of intellectual improvement through the lessons of physical perfection. This means that you are now here in this lifetime to show the rest of us how to be of useful service to others through the practical tasks of daily employment, routine activities, and physical fitness.

While this spiritual agenda may sound like a walk in an astrological park to just about anyone else, when you come into the world with a Virgo degree it goes without saying that yours won't be a popular journey, but then, being the helpful know-it-all never is. As difficult as that is for all of us to endure, it's an impossible fate for you to avoid when you're the one who is karmically qualified to observe the world with a critical eye for detail, or, as we see it, annoyingly compelled to criticize and correct whatever wanders into your field of vision. You can't help it. After all, you earned this degree by brilliantly mastering the analysis and repair of data, policy, procedure, and people, which means you were actually born to ask the difficult questions, find the technical answers, and supply the appropriate facts because you were universally trained to solve our irreparable problems. You know, those messy mistakes and obvious oversights that are carelessly missed or simply ignored by everyone other than you. A daunting task if there ever was one, especially with you on the job and the rest of us under the microscope.

As far as you're concerned, there's really no such thing as a simple problem or a meaningless error. As far as we're concerned, things tend to get a bit more complicated whenever you enter the picture, or, for that matter, the room. There's a reason for that and it happens to be one of the universe's better-kept secrets. You're an idealist. You truly believe that real perfection, like Mt. Everest, is something that not only exists, but can actually be reached. In fact, you're determined to prove this theory or die trying, which, apparently, is when things tend to go downhill for you because, as far as the cosmos is concerned, you're here to reach your noble objectives by demonstrating that excellence, like beauty, is only a realistic concept when it's being used as an inspirational model, not as an impossible standard. That means that although your Virgo diploma celestially certifies you to be a shining example of critical thinking and practical solutions, it also stipulates that you must always strive for perfection without ever being overwhelmed by the inevitable flaws of reality, and that brings us to your very own cosmic conundrum. Mt. Perfection will only be reached when you can accept the unbearable fact that it never was to begin with—that, according to the cosmos, is only achieved when you can admit that some problems have no solutions.

Understandably, when you're shining brightly, you are competent, helpful, conscientious, and effective. With a highly developed sense of correctness and an incredible knack for efficiency, you're impressive in both your ability to work hard and your tendency to adapt easily. Most importantly, you're useful, a genuine worker bee who is capable of patiently enduring all those endless details, tedious responsibilities, and mundane tasks just to achieve that highest degree of excellence.

You also spend a good deal of your life and a whole lot of your time patiently waiting for either the perfect project, the ideal occupation, or the unflawed partner—so much for reality. In fact, whenever that idealism of yours kicks into high gear, your unrealistic goals of perfection can be as destructive to you as they are impossible for us, because the more you try to micromanage everything the less you're satisfied with anything. You then spin your overworked wheels and wallow in self-pity as we watch you become inundated with details, overwhelmed by setbacks, and undermined by your own rigid policies and procedures. Your unacceptable attempt to achieve absolute perfection is then rationalized as an acceptable excuse for doing absolutely nothing. This is when you become less productive, life becomes more frustrating, and your worst fear becomes a reality—the one where fault and failure multiply incessantly as imperfection reigns supreme. Obviously, these are your dark moments—your hypercritical, compulsive, and pessimistic days when we're driven to distraction by your obsessive sense of duty and your never-ending battle to make us painfully aware of who, what, and where the problem is. With a degree in Virgo, it's your purpose.

You're dedicated to the constant search for perfection because you're the master of practical service, a universal trouble-shooter with a sharp and critical awareness that is envied by all and rivaled by none. While your powers of discrimination are remarkable, it should be remembered they are only effective when compassion and respect are responsibly applied to all the people, things, and situations that are unlucky enough to find themselves caught in the crosshairs of your cosmic magnifying glass. After all, you're the one who was trained to make anything right, make everything work, and make all things better, which is why the universe put you in charge of showing us how to strive for your ideal without losing sight of our reality. It's a thankless job, but whoever said fixing the physical flaws of mankind would be easy? Besides, unlike you, the rest of us can't even see them, but then, unlike you, we don't know where to look. Sort of gives new meaning to the term know-it-all, doesn't it?

Cosmic Theme Song: "Nobody Does It Better" by Carly Simon

Sun in Libra

He is the half part of a blessed man,
Left to be finished by such a she;
And she a fair divided excellence,
Whose fullness of perfection lies in him.

—WILLIAM SHAKESPEARE

Karmic Degree: Cooperation, Commitment, and Partnership.
Libra is ruled by Venus, the planet of love, beauty, and pleasure.

As someone who began life while the Sun was moving through Libra, your previous path of soul development was one of intellectual cooperation through the lessons of marriage and partnership. This means that you are now here in this lifetime to show the rest of us how to attract and reciprocate the aesthetic rewards of mutual commitment, meaningful relationships, and social collaboration. Understandably then, you have no choice but to direct your energies outward because, apparently, you're the significant other who is here to enhance the world we live in by giving valuable worth to the personal commitment of one-on-one relationships. No wonder you're always so compelled to focus your attention on the wants and needs of whoever happens to be standing next to you. Being "other-oriented" is actually what you do best. Then again, because the ego-driven energies of the Sun are weakened in this collaborative constellation, being other-obsessed is really what you do most, which is exactly why your own individuality can't help but be continuously compromised. In fact, it's also why your whole earthly existence can't help but be controlled by both the strong sense of justice you happened to inherit and that deep need for symmetry you were forced to develop.

The truth of the matter is, you weren't born to be a loner. Surprisingly, you're not bothered by this and apparently there's a reason for that. This Libra degree was actually earned by learning how to skillfully create and collectively appreciate love, beauty, harmony, and equality. Obviously, not your typical loner pastimes and, definitely, proof positive that you're actually here to personify something that is much more complete and far less lonely than the solitary confinement of overrated individuality. You see, you're here to be a partner, and what's more, you know it. In fact, it's no celestial secret that at times your determination to relate and couple can appear to be almost borderline excessive. It is, but that's only because you were universally trained in the fine art of meaningful collaboration, which, by the way, not only left you secretly addicted to the give-and-take of compromise, but particularly vulnerable to it as well.

That brings us to your very own cosmic conundrum—being yourself—because although your Libra degree karmically qualifies you to eliminate discord, neutralize conflict, and create harmony for others, it also stipulates that you are now officially obligated to do so without losing your own identity in the process. This means that although you're very much in the business of making our lives harmonious and the world more beautiful, self-denial, self-indulgence, and peace at all costs are no longer acceptable methods for getting the job done. Sure, opposing forces must be reconciled, and yes, those beautiful connections still have to be established, but the universe expects you to produce harmony by creating balance in this life, not by giving away power in your own, by doing your best to be a shining example of what real cooperation looks like. That, according to the cosmos, is supposed to look like two separate individuals sharing the same objective, wielding the same power, striving to meet each other's needs without neglecting their own. Yes, it is humanly possible, and no, a cosmic joke would be a lot funnier.

Not surprisingly, you are charming, congenial, objective, and gracious. Most importantly, you're instinctively social and highly effective in your ability to negotiate, mediate, counsel, and articulate. You accommodate like no one else, and we can't help but be impressed each time we watch you effortlessly merge so many different egos into such an incredible example of well-oiled teamwork. Unfortunately, your fixation for cooperative interaction often compels you to chronically compromise your principles or instinctively suppress your own needs just for the sake of either approval, appearance, or that temporary but necessary cease-fire. You can't help it. As far as you're concerned, for every action there has to be an opposite and equal reaction, or at least there should be. It's what you were programmed to believe and trained to implement. Not surprisingly, this remarkable ability to see both sides of any issue and all viewpoints can be as problematic as it is beneficial. It bestows a great tactical advantage and comes in very handy during those critical chess games or frequent military maneuvers, but it's also responsible for your appalling indecisiveness, provocative mixed signals, and annoying changes of mind—those dark and dependent, often manipulative, sometimes superficial, yet always appealing energies of Libra.

We shouldn't be surprised. With a Libra degree, you are the universal ambassador of both beautiful connections and rewarding associations. You will always do whatever it takes to contain a situation because you were born to enhance the quality of our lives by creating harmony in our relationships. Obviously, and with good reason, the universe has chosen you to bring beautiful symmetry into our world. After all, who else has learned to value the so-called spirit of the law as much as its more literal interpretation? Who else instinctively understands that before any alliance can be worthwhile, it must first be equitable? Evidently, you're the one who must demonstrate that a successful relationship can only be achieved by balancing the egos and needs of two separate individuals, primarily because you're the one who knows that it takes two complete halves of one thing to ever make a whole out of anything. Ironically, your only real challenge lies in your ability to remember that one of those complete halves is supposed to be you.

Cosmic Theme Song: "Stand By Me" by Ben E. King

Sun in Scorpio

In nature's infinite book of secrecy, a little I can read.

—WILLIAM SHAKESPEARE

Karmic Degree: Intense Desires, Shared Resources, and Power.
Scorpio is ruled by Pluto, the planet of power and control.

As someone who began life while the Sun was moving through Scorpio, your previous path of soul development was one of emotional transformation through the lessons of intense experiences. This means that you are now here in this lifetime to show the rest of us how to penetrate and master the emotional depths of powerful intimacy, unknown forces, and life and death issues. Obviously, this spiritual agenda is not for the fainthearted because, apparently, you can't avoid getting up close and personal with the formidable forces of nature. There's a reason for that: you were universally trained to be one.

In fact, this Scorpio degree was actually earned by mastering the ability to skillfully access and expertly manipulate the complex energies of power, control, passion, and the unknown. No wonder you were born to unearth what lies beneath the sinister surface, unleash the strength of deeply felt desires, and cosmically collide with danger and disaster. You're the one who must do whatever it takes to skillfully regenerate what is necessary in life and effectively eliminate what is not. No, you're not God, but if you worked a little on those forgiveness issues you could be his understudy, and you know it. You're the celestial shrink who is here to bring about our hand-wringing emotional transformation by way of your nail-biting intestinal fortitude, which is really just another way of describing that passionate sense of purpose you intrinsically engineer to keep yourself obsessively on track and everybody else abusively on edge simply because it is now your karmic responsibility to be a shining example of what you've already learned how to do: survive.

Clearly, crisis management is what you do best, but then, with your karmic credentials, self-preservation is what you do most—aside from intuitively dodging bullets and miraculously moving mountains, of course. This is really not that hard for us to believe once we take into consideration that your amazing willpower is inherently fueled by the incredible intensity of your own deeply held and often desperate desires. Fortunately, you were born with a remarkable understanding that power is nothing more than control and an invaluable survival instinct that keeps you secretly salivating for both. Unfortunately, however, in your attempt to protect everything you hold dear (and in many cases, everything you don't), you tend to use this internal defense system for the sole purpose of denying both the existence and the depth of the one thing that just happens to be your greatest resource: emotional desire. This, according to the cosmos, and unbeknownst to everyone else, is actually your real path to power, not, as you seem to think, your deadly liability. After all, do liabilities move mountains? That's not possible. They do, however, manifest from suppressed passions, like yours, that after having been so quelled for so long are finally forced to seek the lower and more extreme emotional outlets of hatred, paranoia, and obsession. These are outlets, by the way, that can't help but personify your worst fear because they provoke every drastic emotional behavior that reflects it. Loss of control, and what's worse, yours. This isn't just a scary thought, it's an epic irony, because even though this Scorpio degree certifies that no one is more qualified to achieve the physical level of intimacy needed to access hidden power, it also stipulates that no one is more vulnerable to the emotional fear of being controlled by it. That is exactly why the universe taught you to be empowered by your emotions, not manipulated by them, and why you must now move those mountains without destroying our hemisphere.

Understandably, at your brightest, you're shrewd, focused, resourceful, and protective. Most importantly, with piercing insights and fierce determination you're a formidable opponent on any playing field who is frequently underestimated by those around you. As the master of dangerous secrets and emotional sacrifice, you prefer it that way. That is, until your deep fear of emotional vulnerability rears its ugly head, bringing your unfounded paranoia and chronic distrust along with it. This is when you become your controlling, manipulative, and uncompromising worst as you hide behind defensive walls and compulsively transform your psychological strengths of intuition, devotion, and courage into the emotional weapons of jealousy, vengeance, and obsession. Your most destructive offense then becomes your most likely defense as every drastic weapon in your psychological arsenal is strategically employed to ensure that your so-called enemies are totally annihilated at least one full week before they even get around to knowing you exist. Militarily speaking, that's the scorched earth policy. Emotionally speaking, it's your standard operating procedure. Who's surprised?

With a degree in Scorpio, you're the universal survivor who, like the cyclical forces of nature, must now be the personification of internal power. No wonder you're constantly compelled to seek the intensity of intimate liaisons and meaningful experiences. You were trained to reveal the deep reserves that are available to all of us by demonstrating to anyone who's allowed to get close enough that our most powerful resource actually lies in the untapped potency of nature's strongest principle: human desire. Sure, we can expect a good deal of fallout along the way, but don't worry, putting out fires is your karmic responsibility. So is starting them. Survival 101 was your cosmic classroom, which explains how you learned to generate new beginnings from the ruins of deathlike endings and why you're always the one still standing when the smoke clears. Evidently it's now your universal purpose to teach the rest of us where to find our own power, but that's only the beginning. Your real mission and greatest challenge is being a masterful earthly example of how to use it wisely.

Cosmic Theme Song: "Stayin' Alive" by the Bee Gees

Sun in Sagittarius

There are more things in heaven and earth, Horatio,
Than are dreamt of in your philosophy.

—WILLIAM SHAKESPEARE

Karmic Degree: Truth, Knowledge, and Enlightenment.
Sagittarius is ruled by Jupiter, the planet of luck and expansion.

As someone who began life while the Sun was moving through Sagittarius, your previous path of soul development was one of intellectual growth through the lessons of physical expansion. This means that you are now here in this lifetime to show the rest of us how to broaden our minds as well as our horizons through those challenging frontiers of global communications, higher education, moral philosophies, and distant places. Congratulations. You've been issued the Lewis and Clark meets Dudley Do-Right of spiritual agendas, otherwise known as a Sagittarian degree, and otherwise earned for being able to question the unanswered and explore the unknown while discovering the truth and saving the day. No wonder you must courageously defend idealistic principles and passionately uphold starry-eyed possibilities. You're the cosmic crusader who is here to inspire us all with our unlimited opportunities by enlightening the world with your deep philosophic beliefs. Now, aside from impatiently overlooking details and recklessly disregarding consequences, there is really nothing you do better. In fact, this degree was earned by learning how to romantically pursue and masterfully promote truth, knowledge, justice, and adventure. This is why you can't help but repeatedly throw proverbial caution to the wind and successfully defy the unfavorable odds.

You were trained to perpetually push the outside of every boring envelope. Evidently, you have no choice but to challenge the limits of your intellectual, physical, and spiritual boundaries because, obviously, it's your karmic responsibility to move beyond them. Fortunately, you're well equipped for this mission, as the universe has armed you with a noble sense of justice and a spirited sense of adventure. Unfortunately, it doesn't provide a cape, but no problem, you've got heart. In fact, the sheer magnitude of idealistic zeal pumping through your veins at any given moment is not only enough to fuel your own heroic convictions and courageous campaigns, but those of Joan of Arc, Abraham Lincoln, and even Batman. Come to think of it, that is exactly the kind of tag team it would take to keep all that devoted enthusiasm of yours from spiraling into self-righteous fanaticism every time you go looking for purpose in all the wrong places. After all, there are just so many opportunities to vigorously crusade for just causes or faithfully defend the underdog before your passion finds itself fresh out of lofty options and forced to settle for plan B, the one that compels you to save us from ourselves by simply adjusting our moral compass with your moral superiority or, as the universe sees it, the beginning of your end.

That's because while your Sagittarius degree certifies that no one is more karmically qualified to be a shining example of inspired enlightenment, it also stipulates that your superhero status is totally off the table the minute the cosmos catches you abandoning your continuous search for knowledge, or worse, recklessly applying the truth. Evidently, you're now expected to share your wisdom and circulate your beliefs without dismissing conflicting viewpoints, ignoring opposing opinions, or promoting only your own findings. In short, you must always aspire to know it all without ever appearing to be one. Hmmm. Looks like you may need that cape after all.

Not surprisingly, at your brightest you're optimistic, principled, generous, and insightful. Most importantly, you adapt readily to change and infuse everyone around you with your passion for ideas and your enthusiasm for adventure. No wonder you often feel guided by divine intuition and protected by lucky circumstances. You are. You're also instinctively entertaining and innately fun-loving, which is why you thrive on both the competition of intellectual challenge and the sporting fun of any kind of gamesmanship.

On the dark side, however, your immense appetite for freedom and even bigger distaste for moderation compels you to stubbornly reject everyone else's opinions for no other reason than that you refuse to be restricted by anyone else's limits. This is when you scatter yourself too thin and push everyone else too far as you impulsively aim too high and recklessly promise too much. Overwhelmed in a backlash of unfinished projects and forgotten appointments, you then desperately attempt to save face by pompously ignoring the intellectual opposition, arbitrarily moving the moral goal-posts and self-righteously refusing to play by any other belief system. Incredibly, the world failed to live up to your expectations.

In reality, it simply failed to follow your rule book. But then, with all those exceptions and inconsistencies of yours, who can? Obviously, not even you, and there's a reason for that. With a degree in Sagittarius, you're here to push your worldly wisdom by pushing your earthly limits. You're the universal seeker of truth who has already learned that knowledge, like growth, is only possible through the unlimited experiences of intellectual, spiritual, and physical freedom, which is why you've been universally authorized to follow your heart and live by your principles. It's also why you've been endowed with the keys to enlightenment and the promise of a global pulpit. Through your example, we must learn the power of possibilities, because through your example we must be inspired to go further, and make no mistake about it, with your wisdom ringing in our ears, we will. In fact, it's no coincidence that you've been universally endowed with more than enough of the only thing that anyone needs to make even the most impossible dreams come true: faith. You're here to teach us that our dreams, like our truths, really do have the power to take us anywhere if we believe in them, and you will—assuming, of course, that when it comes to your own, you remember to practice what you preach.

Cosmic Theme Song: "Daydream Believer" by the Monkees

Sun in Capricorn

But if it be a sin to covet honor,
I am the most offending soul alive.

—WILLIAM SHAKESPEARE

Karmic Degree: Career, Responsibility, and Reputation.
Capricorn is ruled by Saturn, the planet of limitation and discipline.

As someone who began life while the Sun was moving through Capricorn, your previous path of soul development was one of material success through the lessons of worldly ambition. This means that you are now here in this lifetime to show the rest of us how to manage and master the official responsibilities of parental authority, professional career, and public reputation. Welcome to the astrological equivalent of great expectations in a goldfish bowl. What else would you call a spiritual agenda that expects you to aim high and work hard so that you can get rich and be great, but only after you've officially paid your dues in the eyes of the world and yet sometime before you've legally lost your mind in the eyes of your heirs? Mission impossible? Absolutely, but cheer up. There's much more than just a cosmic grindstone out there with your name on it. There's a powerful promise that goes with it. It's called the ladder of success, and the universal buzz is that you're going places. Which is why you can't help but be inspired by a sense of purpose and focused on specific goals. You're the ground-floor nobody who is here to establish your position in the outside world by becoming a powerful somebody in your own particular field. Sure, you must assume responsibility and grapple for control because, one way or another, you're supposed to reach the top, and that, according to the cosmos, means starting at the bottom.

Not to worry. If anyone can climb their ambitious way up the practical rungs of organized structure, it's someone who was universally trained to make it. You. In fact, you actually received this Capricorn degree by skillfully earning and effectively utilizing power, authority, respect, and status. No wonder you can achieve what no one else can and succeed where others have failed. You simply have what no one else has: the inside track. This is why you were born knowing how the system works. It's also why, on those dark and more political days, you know how to work the system. While that's usually to your material advantage, it's often at your spiritual expense, which, sooner or later, just ends up inhibiting your professional success. It has to.

That's because even though this Capricorn degree certifies that you are the one who is now karmically qualified to be a shining example of accomplished leadership in any field, it also stipulates that your success and happiness will never be experienced by manipulating the rules, abusing responsibility, or bypassing authority in any way. Evidently, the universe expects you to personify professional achievement and demonstrate material success by dutifully working within the established order for the responsible sake of all concerned. Obviously, your only rule on this cosmic playing field is a universal one: the ends can no longer justify your means, even if you are going places.

Not surprisingly, no one is more responsible, organized, disciplined, and industrious. Most importantly, you get things done. You're determined to succeed and in spite of the most difficult tasks and demanding superiors, you always manage to aspire to the best office in the company, the best seat in the house, and even the best space in the parking lot. That is why you never fail to respect anyone else who does the same.

As a natural executive, you consistently impress the powers that be with your outstanding ability to be both an effective team leader and a valuable team player. Essentially, there is really nothing you can't accomplish. Unfortunately, however, there is often nothing you won't do to accomplish it. Needless to say, from our envious perspective, this powerful drive can only be ruthless ambition. From your unworthy one, it's more like a deep sense of inadequacy. What few people understand is that you harbor a profound fear of failure that actually feeds on control and prompts your rigid, opportunistic, and even merciless approach to your objectives. In fact, the reason you have great difficulty asking for help or admitting mistakes is simply because you refuse to appear weak or ineffective to anyone. Instead, you coldly use whomever you must and capitalize on whatever you can to selfishly achieve whatever you desire. You then become domineering, obsessive, calculating, and materialistic. We become amazed when you arrogantly disregard the importance of appropriate boundaries, the necessity of responsible limits, or the value of reliable structures. We really shouldn't be amazed. With a degree in Capricorn, success is not an option, it's your purpose. No matter what your profession, you'll always be committed to the ambitious pursuit of money, honor, position, and authority, because no matter what you do you'll always be responsible for illuminating the power they wield in the outside world. You're the one who was chosen to teach us the universal principle of "we get what we earn" because you're the one who has mastered the curriculum of earthly fame and material fortune. That means you really have no choice but to get out where we can see you and start scaling those prestigious heights and conquering those prominent pinnacles. You're universally obligated to demonstrate the high price of status and the overwhelming responsibility of power. Impossible demands will be made of you, but only because impossible goals are waiting to be realized. Besides, unlike us, the universe has endowed you with an unlimited supply of the only element that actually fuels professional desire and guarantees your triumphant climb to success: ambition. Apparently, your only real challenge on the way up that ladder is to keep yourself from becoming blinded by it.

Cosmic Theme Song: "Respect" by Aretha Franklin

Sun in Aquarius

Commit the oldest sins the newest kind of ways.

—WILLIAM SHAKESPEARE

Karmic Degree: Social Reform and Creative Ingenuity.
Aquarius is ruled by Uranus, the planet of change and originality.

As someone who began life while the Sun was moving through Aquarius, your previous path of soul development was one of intellectual individuality through the lessons of social participation. This means that you are now here in this lifetime to show the rest of us how to stimulate and inspire those humanitarian ideals of progressive thinking, universal brotherhood, and social reform. No wonder you can't help but infuse everyone around you with exciting possibilities and original alternatives. You're the idealistic visionary who is here to make our world a better place by waiting until we all get comfortable and then somehow making it a different place. If this spiritual agenda is starting to sound a little revolutionary, that's only because it is. In fact, your Aquarian degree was not only earned by learning how to brilliantly envision any kind of change, friendship, invention, and tomorrow, but by showing the rest of us how to collectively provoke them as well. That is why you never have any other choice but to insist on freedom, reject convention, and demand innovation on a regular basis. It's what you were universally trained to do.

Understandably, then, as far as you're concerned, upsetting the status quo is always essential to finding a better way. Even more understandably, though, as far as we're concerned, the status could never be anywhere near quo whenever you're around. After all, how could it be when you habitually adopt lifestyles that are counter to current trends, continuously embrace anything off-beat or unique, and rarely appear to look, act, or feel uncomfortable in strange situations? Even the friendships you find to be the most stimulating are usually with the people we just find to be, well, the most unusual.

The good news is, you have no problem being the universal maverick, which is why you're really quite good at it. That's because you not only like being different, you actually take great pride in it—in fact, maybe a little too much pride. This brings us to the bad news. Evidently, your ego and identity get so invested in your intellect that you can't help but become willfully rebellious whenever your radical ideas, broad-minded attitudes, and unconventional associations are not happily endorsed by everyone. You may want to brace yourself for this one because here comes your cosmic hurdle. You see, while it's true your Aquarian degree certifies that you're now karmically qualified to be our shining example of independent thinking, it also stipulates that you must do so without stubbornly rejecting the thoughts and opinions of others just because they're not your own. Talk about universal hardball. Apparently, your revolutions are supposed to have a higher purpose than just your intellectual pride—like the betterment of humankind, for example.

Consequently, when you're tapping into your brightest energies, you're impressively objective and extraordinarily progressive. Most importantly, you're an idealist with a unique gift for dealing with all types of people from every walk of life, a real individual who easily grants others the freedom to be themselves and genuinely likes to see everyone happy. At your darkest, however, you're just as capable of being unpredictably stubborn, detached, eccentric, and disruptive. On these particularly contrary days, the pleasure you derive from basking in chaos and rebellion is only surpassed by the secret satisfaction you obtain from being able to create it. That is when your obsessive fear of being just like everyone else provokes you to obstinately ignore tradition and arrogantly inflate your own importance while brilliantly posing as an expert. You then aim to shock and manage to hit your mark as you become surprisingly unreasonable, and we become, well, unreasonably surprised. We shouldn't be. With your creative individuality calling the shots, in one way or another you will always manage to separate yourself from the masses. You must. It's your purpose—a purpose that is obviously reflected in your gift for visionary concepts and your aptitude for scientific principles. Why else would you be so intrigued by everything avant garde or so compelled by anything state of the art? Perhaps because being mindful of tomorrow is more than just an interesting pastime or even a pastime interest. It's your karmic responsibility because it used to be your cosmic curriculum.

With a degree in Aquarius, you can't help but be instilled with the spirit of humanity when you've been trained in the school of social progress. You're the one who must strive to be different because you're the one who has already learned that our strength as a society really depends on our uniqueness as individuals. Of course you refuse to conform—you can't help it. You firmly believe that it's up to you to show each and every one of us how and when to tap into our own creative genius. It is. Besides, on some instinctive level you know that it's only by becoming our brilliant best as individuals that we ever become a more evolved and powerful group of people. Unlike us, you're aware of the much bigger picture: the collective consciousness of humankind. Unlike us, you really belong to another time: the future. No wonder we watch in awe as you undauntedly swim upstream, willingly take the road less traveled, and confidently march to the beat of a different drummer. The universe has chosen you to inspire all of us to get out there and do the same—and you will. In fact, with a degree in Aquarius, your only real challenge lies in your ability to accept the fact that, when that time comes, your idea of a different drummer is not necessarily the better one. Hard to swallow, isn't it?

Cosmic Theme Song: "My Life" by Billy Joel

Sun in Pisces

Some rise by sin, and some by virtue fall.

—WILLIAM SHAKESPEARE

Karmic Degree: Emotional Healing and Compassionate Service.
Pisces is ruled by Neptune, the planet of mystery and illusion.

As someone who began life while the Sun was moving through Pisces, your previous path of soul development was one of emotional wholeness through the lessons of psychological healing. This means that you are now here in this lifetime to show the rest of us how to be of compassionate service to others through the idealistic concepts of unconditional faith, creative imagination, and psychological health. Obviously, this spiritual agenda is not for lesser mortals because, apparently, you've been universally trained to instinctively "seek unity with all that is," or indiscriminately merge with anything in your path. You must. You're the idealist who is here to seek a greater perfection than the real world is capable of producing, which, aside from turning the other cheek and sugar-coating disappointment, is really what you do best. You can't help that you're the one who always sees the good hidden in the bad and always hears the truth buried in the lie. You're the one who was cosmically conditioned to always find the hope somewhere in the hopelessness. In fact, this Pisces degree was brilliantly earned by learning how to dissolve divisive boundaries, rehabilitate harsh concepts of reality, and create alternate states of consciousness. You believe in winning lottery tickets and storybook endings. Miracles are your specialty because trust is your karmic responsibility. Of course, the rose-colored glasses don't hurt either, which is exactly what your remarkable faith, incredible imagination, and unlimited compassion become when they work together for the sole purpose of allowing you to see exactly what you want to see every time the world doesn't live up to your starry-eyed standards.

Now, you're probably wondering when we get to the hard part, which means it's time to take off the glasses and face up to the fact that you can't heal the grim realities of life if you're actually using a rosier escape route like unconditional love, denial, or addiction as a way to bypass them. Because when you do, it's never for long and it's always with consequences. Yours. As hard as it is to believe, your pain is not what you're here for—our healing is. In fact, according to the cosmos, it's time for you to remember that somewhere on your soul's hazy journey down the yellow brick road you agreed to inspire us by relieving our sorrow, not by reliving or avoiding yours. This means that although your Pisces degree certifies that you are karmically qualified to provide compassionate healing for the whole of human suffering, it also stipulates that you must now be a shining example of pain-free, conscious awareness while doing so. So much for cosmic crutches. Evidently your devotion to psychological health and your obsession with emotional bliss must now be used to produce a therapeutic "high" or an emotional nirvana for someone other than yourself, perhaps the helpless or the hopeless. That's right, this is the hard part. In your contract, it's called the reality clause.

Understandably, at your brightest, you're incredibly imaginative, impressively charitable, and foolishly idealistic. Most importantly, you're extremely compassionate and not afraid to break the rules when a more humane approach is needed, and while your profound intuition and deep sensitivity leave you highly susceptible to just about every altered state of consciousness, they also instill a propensity for anything relating to the spiritual or mystical.

This powerful need to connect and merge, however, makes it almost impossible for you to maintain your emotional equilibrium and sometimes even your own identity. In fact, pretending is something you do rather well with this solar degree because mastering the fine art of make-believe is a Pisces prerequisite. This not only explains your instinctive ability to just become someone else whenever the frustrations of being yourself prove to be too overwhelming, but also that annoying facility you have of appearing so delusional, deceitful, or spineless on a lot of other occasions as well. These are your dark days, when you unconsciously sabotage your own agenda and occasionally undermine ours by either avoiding the unpleasant work you should be doing, enabling the difficult soul you should be saving, or just ignoring the painful problem you should be solving. With a degree in Pisces, what did we expect? After all, you're the universal medic who is dedicated to the emotional well-being of mankind. As noble as that is, with all that empathy coursing through your veins, the lines between rescuer and victim are bound to get a little blurred once in awhile.

The good news is: you have choices. You can use all that creative sensitivity as your means of living up to this noble calling or, sadly, as your "go to" excuse for falling victim to it. Either way, you will serve. It's your purpose. Your choice however, is whether you will inspire us by providing the compassionate support you promised to others, or burden us by becoming the emotional cripple you agreed to help. It's that simple. You're here to make the world a little less terrible and a lot more tolerable, which is why you always have such infinite faith in the powers that be. You are one. It is also the reason you were universally endowed with such divine powers of unconditional love, abstract awareness, and psychic insight. You have healing to do. In fact, on some level you even know that you're supposed to attract every psychological casualty and emotional victim who desperately needs compassion. Apparently, your only real challenge down here in the real world is remembering that you're not supposed to be one of them, which, regrettably, brings us to the bad news. Rose-colored glasses are prohibited.

Cosmic Theme Songs: "Imagine" by John Lennon and "Margaritaville" by Jimmy Buffett

4

The Sun House: Your Karmic Calling

Oft expectation fails, and most oft there
Where most it promises.

—WILLIAM SHAKESPEARE

As you can see, reflecting the qualities of your Sun sign is not the difficult part of your contract with the universe. After all, just being who you are isn't hard to do. Applying yourself is, which brings us to the second half of the solar clause in your contract and, for that reason, the twelve houses of the natal chart.

First, however, a few boring, but necessary facts. Just as that celestial beltway, the ecliptic, is made up of twelve different constellations we call signs, the birth chart is also divided into twelve different sections astrologers call houses. Just as each constellation depicts a specific area of the sky above, each house in the natal chart represents a specific area of life down below. Now. because the birth chart was designed to serve as a celestial snapshot of the day you were born, it was purposely configured so that each one of the houses in it would reflect an approximate two-hour period of that day. This is done by casting the chart so the cusp of the 1st house reflects the eastern horizon at the exact moment of daybreak on that morning (sometime between 6 and 8 am); and the cusp of the 7th house mirrors the western horizon at the exact moment of sunset on that evening (usually between 6 and 8 pm).

With these exact times set in place as horizon anchors, every one of the twelve houses on this birth wheel ends up representing not only a specific two-hour period of the Sun's journey around the Earth that day, but the actual section of the sky that the Sun was occupying while it was making that journey. At 12 o'clock noon the Sun would be directly overhead and at 12 o'clock midnight it would be directly below the earth. Therefore, because the Sun had to be breaking, climbing, falling, or setting in one of those twelve sections of the sky at the exact moment of your birth, it would have to be reflected as doing so in one of the twelve houses of the birth chart as well. Your birth chart: as above, so below. I hope this makes it a little easier to understand why your birth time is so critical to your horoscope and so crucial to your contract. It's the only way to determine which of these twelve houses your Sun was astrologically positioned in at the moment of your birth, and, because of that, the only way to know what area of life your solar degree is universally contracted to in this lifetime.

Not surprisingly then, if there's one piece of the astrological puzzle you need to have, it's your Sun house. Because while every house in the natal chart will, at times, be challenging, the house your Sun occupied at the moment of your first independent breath will always be the most frustrating. That's because the areas of life it represents will always be the most demanding. They have to be. While your Sun sign is your karmic degree (that part of your contract that validates your solar greatness and illuminates to the outside world just how you're karmically qualified to make your mark in this lifetime), your Sun house is the clause in your contract that unequivocally identifies just where you agreed to make it. Therefore, on the bright side, your Sun house represents the field of human life where you can expect to shine because it reveals exactly where you promised to hit that spiritual home run.

On the dark side, however, this house also represents the areas of life where the cosmos expects you to show up for the games, play by the rules, and swing for the fences like the pro you were trained to be. Yes, the one you agreed to become, not just on those good-luck days when you feel like it, but on those bad-hair days when you don't. Unless, of course, you don't mind forfeiting your spot on the field and your shot at success. After all, it is your promise, your consequences. Besides, this house is not supposed to be easy. Being brilliant never is, at least not when it requires keeping a cosmic promise to literally get up every day and figuratively break a real human sweat. This, by the way, is more than just the best way to honor your solar commitment. It's the only way to access your maximum potential. That's right. There's absolutely no way you will ever be able to reap the universal rewards of success and fulfillment without *doing* the hard work of being a major player in your Sun house. In fact, every time you choose to do something less strenuous in that house, like perhaps nothing, the universe takes it personally, as it should. This is usually when your ego takes a hit and your life takes a dive. When you neglect the responsibilities of your Sun house, you're not only sidestepping your personal commitment, you're actually bypassing your designated potential, causing you to unhappily plummet straight into the astrological abyss of deep solar dissatisfaction. This is not to be confused with any other type of earthly discontent because, when it comes to the dark side of an untapped Sun, the dissatisfaction is so deep it actually alienates even your strongest supporters by compelling you to habitually whine and complain about all the things you never get from your Sun house, while even more habitually making no human attempt to work for any of them. In short, Lazy Sun Syndrome, and yes, you may already be afflicted.

For instance, if your 10th house Sun is not out there in the public eye doing a brilliant interpretation of responsible leadership, you can be sure it's only because you're somewhere inside your own private hell complaining about the authority you always fail to achieve and the recognition you never seem to get. If, on the other inharmonious hand, you're the one weeping and moaning about relationships that are too difficult to sustain and partnerships that are impossible to achieve, you can be sure that your 7th house Sun isn't doing its best to be a shining example of balanced cooperation at its finest. Who do you suppose spends a good deal of their time griping about resources that aren't there, banks that don't come through, and partners who are emotionally, financially, or spiritually bankrupt? The 8th house Sun whose powerful paranoia keeps them from doing their very own share of the deep sharing work. It doesn't matter if that 2nd house Sun of yours has agreed to show the rest of us how to make money and accumulate wealth, if a reliable value system has not been developed, your lazy Sun complaints about high prices and insufficient earnings are old and annoying. If your 4th house Sun is constantly crying about the lack of stability on the domestic scene, it's a pretty sure bet that you're the one dominating the household by not doing the hard work of giving others the psychological foundation you promised, or worse, the emotional security they need. Get the picture? Being a powerful influence means more than just wielding authority and dishing out expertise, it means using them to make an impressive difference by being an outstanding individual. That, according to the cosmos, is more than just interpreting your solar placement, it's living up to it. It's stepping up to your karmic calling.

So what if personal fulfillment could be universally guaranteed by just rolling up your earthly sleeves and doing the required heavy lifting of your Sun house. Would it be worth a try? Of course it would. At the very least, it would have to be worth the cost of all those therapy sessions, self-help classes, and overpriced calls to the psychic hotline. After all, if hitting one out of the park was simply a matter of showing up on the right field, wouldn't you want to know where it was? Who wouldn't? Knowledge is power, isn't it? Besides, as you're about to find out, when it comes to the solar clause in your natal contract, ignorance has never been bliss. Just ask anyone with a 3rd house Sun. Or, better yet, find your own Sun house in the birth chart, and get busy. Chances are you're out there every day overlooking the most direct route to your much better life.

That's because while you already know that the power of your natal Sun is always available to you through the sign it was traveling through at the moment of your birth, what you probably have yet to realize is that its promise is only available to you through the house that it occupies in your birth chart. That is why this compelling influence is called your karmic calling, the second half of the solar clause in your personal contract with the universe—the one that illuminates your very reason for existence. Look no further. Your Sun house is, without question, the astrological house of your human happiness and your earthly prosperity. Quite literally, it's what the cosmos, in all its infinite wisdom, says you were born to do.

Sun in the 1st House

With the Sun positioned in the 1st house of your natal chart, you have agreed to apply the hard-earned expertise of your Sun sign to the personal development of the individual self. This means that you must now use the power of your solar degree to discover your character, explore your persona, and express your own identity. Evidently, you have no choice but to achieve success through the strength and confidence of your own independent actions because, ultimately, you were born to inspire ours. This is exactly why you seem to experience nothing but universal green lights whenever you direct those egotistical energies of yours to the individual performance, personal growth, or physical appearance aspects of life—especially your own. With a 1st house Sun, you're supposed to be dripping with self-awareness and committed to self-improvement, which explains all the self-promotion. That's because showing off is actually mandatory with this placement, but you knew that. After all, your soul did make a promise to devote this earthly existence to the fearless advancement of ego and self. There is a highly coveted position of leadership in it for you when you do—something that's never going to happen if you're patiently standing in someone else's shadow or constantly clinging to the inconspicuous sidelines. No wonder your life proves to be very unsatisfying anytime you allow your activities and ambitions to become even slightly dependent on others—or worse, you find yourself stuck in a group on some do-nothing committee that must follow directions and work as a team. Yes, death would be easier, but that's only because you promised the cosmos that your self-esteem would be earned by you, and it will. It's a celestial certainty. With your Sun pledged to the house of impossible ideals, the universe won't let you get away with anything less than noble behavior. This one's nonnegotiable. Evidently, self-improvement is only possible through the hard work of living up to high standards and even higher hopes. This is exactly why you can expect to encounter quite a bit of conflict, challenge, and lots of opposition as you pursue your highly charged purpose on this self-absorbed path to your powerful potential. Everyone knows you can do it—just watch out for flying glass.

Your Lazy Sun Syndrome Complaints: "I'm not getting enough freedom"; "Everyone else has too much."

Sun in the 2nd House

With the Sun positioned in the 2nd house of your natal chart, you have agreed to apply the hard-earned expertise of your Sun sign to the physical acquisition of material wealth. This means you must now use the power of your solar degree to do nothing more than earn money, accumulate assets, and achieve tangible results with nothing less than honorable dealings and ethical practices as your standard operating procedures. This is a tough one, because that's really nothing but a virtual impossibility if you haven't first developed a reliable value system. Cosmically speaking, that would be a personal set of guiding principles that inspires you to attract on a physical level whatever it is you consider to be worthwhile on the material one. Sure, you get to appraise property, appreciate value, and allocate funds, but that's only because accessing your maximum potential depends on your ability to generate a standard of excellence you can be proud of, not just those profitable results you're so fond of. That is why you positively shine whenever you direct your energies to anything that encourages the masterful management of whatever personal resources just happen to be at your disposal, a category that happens to include yourself. With your Sun committed to the "show me the money" house of the natal chart, it's no celestial secret that your biggest financial asset and greatest personal resource is you.

In fact, you've actually been blessed with great earning power in this lifetime because you've pledged yourself to the hard work of deserving it. While that's a deed more universally known as rolling up your somewhat self-indulgent sleeves and becoming the brilliant source of your own independent income, it's more likely to be accomplished through the painful process of accepting responsibility for your own economic exploits. No wonder life becomes so depressingly insufficient every time you're tempted to succumb to the tight-fisted, greedy, and selfish pitfalls of the physical world, or worse, to those unscrupulous financial ones. After all, you did make a promise to devote your earthly efforts to the constructive and beneficial use of your own material resources. A promise worth keeping because the pay-off is definitely a possession worth having. What is it? The physical gratification that comes with building a tangible sense of your own security or, as it's more commonly known, self-worth.

Your Lazy Sun Syndrome Complaints: "Their prices are too high"; "My salary is too low."

Sun in the 3rd House

With the Sun positioned in the 3rd house of your natal chart, you have agreed to apply the hard-earned expertise of your Sun sign to the fundamental development of the intellect: ours—through the exhilarating experience of the immediate environment: yours. This means that you must now use the power of your solar degree to engage our minds in the actual learning process by stimulating our curiosity in the collective neighborhood, which is really just another way of saying you must expose us to that intricate web of interesting information and provocative people that seem to enhance our world by just inhabiting your zip code. Evidently, achieving your maximum potential depends on your ability to thoroughly investigate and skillfully circulate whatever happens to wander into your cosmic coordinates or, for that matter, your mind. Then, with your Sun committed to the quantum classroom of the 3rd house, your astrological assignment is to generate brilliant ideas and discover newsworthy information because you made a promise to personify the universal principle that knowledge is power. That means devoting this lifetime to the very hard work of demonstrating it, which also includes developing the necessary skills to deliver it.

No wonder you have such an incredible nose for news, such an intuitive way with words, and such an instinctual knack for networking. It's also why you can't help but shine with such blinding authority when it comes to almost any aspect of communication, education, commerce, or transportation. That is, until the cosmos catches you trying to flex a little mental muscle by arrogantly dominating and pompously dismissing the very thoughts and conversations you're supposed to be stimulating, or worse, distorting them, which is exactly when your life becomes unsatisfying, the environment becomes monotonous, and, as far as we're concerned, you become both. You see, although our mental development is truly dependent on your powerful connections in the neighborhood, your own personal success depends on your ability to get out there and become the most impressive person in it. That means you can sit back and wait for that outstanding sibling, neighbor, merchant, or teacher to make a brilliant impact on the local community by bringing their powerful message to a theatre near you, or you can live up to your soul's 3rd house promise and become that person yourself.

Your Lazy Sun Syndrome Complaints: "No one ever tells me anything"; "They think they should know everything?"

Sun in the 4th House

With the Sun positioned in the 4th house of your natal chart, you have agreed to apply the hard-earned expertise of your Sun sign to the instinctual pursuit of domestic stability for the fundamental purpose of emotional security. This means that you must now use the power of your solar degree to infuse each and every one of us with a strong sense of who we are by instilling in us a profound feeling of where we belong. No problem. You've been blessed with the necessary insight to know what it is we need, even when we don't. This is exactly why you always seem to experience nothing but universal blue skies and celestial sunshine whenever you direct your somewhat self-absorbed energies to the hard work of either creating the intimacy, providing the care, or establishing the support that is an earthly essential to the emotional survival of others. Apparently, accessing your maximum potential depends on your instinctive ability to nurture ours—not, as you'd like us to believe, on whom, what, and where you came from. With your Sun committed to the natal needs of the 4th house, you were born to assume the metaphorical responsibility of nourishing our emotional roots and building our psychological foundations, but only because you're the one who literally agreed to preserve and protect every aspect of home, hearth, and family. Because of that you can't help but shine with impressive dedication whenever you apply yourself to any area of Mom, apple pie, and country. That is, until your compulsion to care for those around you becomes an obsession to control them, like when your fierce territorial instincts and deep family pride compel you to dominate or smother the very people, things, and property you're supposed to be cultivating—or worse, allows you to spoil them. This is usually what sets the stage for all those frequent family hostilities and so many frustrating real-estate fiascoes. You made a planetary pledge to give us roots, not clip our wings. In fact, as a child, you were greatly influenced by an outstanding someone who had the powerful ability to either illuminate your life on the domestic scene or dominate it. Not surprisingly, as an adult, you now have both the power and the potential to do the same.

Your Lazy Sun Syndrome Complaints: "My family tries to dominate me"; "My mother won't support me."

Sun in the 5th House

With the Sun positioned in the 5th house of your natal chart, you have agreed to apply the hard-earned expertise of your Sun sign to the joyful expression of the creative self. This means that you must now use the power of your solar degree to celebrate life, generate happiness, and demonstrate leadership through no other method than the brilliant display of your own creative talent, and for no other purpose than inspiring the rest of us to do the same. No wonder your planetary pursuit of pleasure is always somehow achieved through the creative use of your mind, body, and spirit, and always somewhat invigorated by the blinding glare of the competitive spotlight.

Apparently, accessing your maximum potential depends on your ability to enrich the lives of those around you while playfully reaping the fruits of your own ingenious labors, and wowing the world in the noteworthy process. Tough assignment, but then, with your Sun pledged to the "look Ma, no hands" house of the horoscope, you can't help but shine with celestial superiority whenever you direct your egotistical energies to the fun and games of getting our attention, primarily because you're now committed to the pomp and pageantry of winning our respect or, as you tend to think of it, applause. This is something you rarely have difficulty earning whenever your powerful passion for children, romance, and entertainment happens to position you in the spotlight and us in the front row. After all, you're here to provide the childlike spirit that encourages artistic individuality, not the childish egotism that spoils and suppresses it—or worse, wastes it.

With a 5th house Sun, you promised the cosmos that you would leave your own individual mark on the world, which explains why you were an outstanding child from the moment you came into it, and why, as an adult, you must work hard to inspire others as a talented teacher, actor, or performer before leaving it, unless, of course, you prefer to experience the ego-deflating 5th house alternatives of embarrassing investments and disappointing offspring. It seems to be magnificent; your natal Sun must first be responsible, making it cosmically clear that although it may be your universal birthright to show off, it's an impossible feat for even you to accomplish without first showing up.

Your Lazy Sun Syndrome Complaints: "My leadership is never recognized"; "I'm always stuck with all the responsibility."

Sun in the 6th House

With the Sun positioned in the 6th house of your natal chart, you have agreed to apply the hard-earned expertise of your Sun sign to the practical duty of physical service. This means that you must now use the power of your solar degree to somehow improve the mundane existence of our daily lives through the somewhat routine responsibilities of your daily grind. No wonder you feel like a professional slave to duty. You are. In fact, on some level, you're actually convinced that you were only brought into this world to devote your mind and muscle to those tiresome tasks of everyday living that are so desperately needed by everyone else. You were, but that's only because in some little corner of our daily drudgery lies an occupational niche with your name on it, some type of much-needed service in an ordinary field that just happens to be your very own celestial specialty. This is mostly because it happens to require some kind of technical talent and/or physical know-how that was previously perfected by you and must now be impressively practiced on us, without all the chronic complaints and neurotic nit-picking, of course. The tough stuff is actually what you're here to do, not as you seem to think, like.

With your Sun committed to the solar sweatshop of the 6th house, you're not only pledged to the hard work of providing a useful service to others, you're also stuck with the awesome responsibility of being good at it, primarily because you've agreed to the planetary purpose of being good for us. This explains why you never have any difficulty blinding us with your brilliance when it comes to matters of health, nutrition, hygiene, or fitness, and, unfortunately, every difficulty avoiding those 6th house headaches of overbearing coworkers, debilitating illnesses, and long periods of unemployment whenever you don't. You were born to shine through our efficiency. Therefore, your personal success actually lies somewhere in those thankless chores no one else wants to do, those broken things no one else cares to fix, and the midnight oil no one else likes to burn. After all, you're the one who made a promise to improve our way of living, which, apparently, just can't be accomplished without working for yours.

Your Lazy Sun Syndrome Complaints: "I always have to do everything"; "No one else knows how to do anything."

Sun in the 7th House

With the Sun positioned in the 7th house of your natal chart, you have agreed to apply the hard-earned expertise of your Sun sign to the mutual commitment of close personal relationships. This means that you must now use the power of your solar degree to responsibly celebrate others, brilliantly neutralize adversaries, and impressively establish alliances. No wonder you find it necessary to measure yourself by the status and value of your partnerships. On some level, you're instinctively aware that you just can't achieve success and happiness all by yourself. You can't. In fact, accessing your maximum potential not only depends on your willingness to relate to those around you effectively, but on your ability to do so objectively. With your Sun pledged to the symmetrical spirit of the 7th house, you're actually committed to the collaborative give-and-take of shared cooperation. That is why the universe tends to provide an obstacle-free path for you every time you direct your earthly efforts to any aspect of social enrichment, contractual agreement, or public relations. Not surprisingly, being so other-oriented does have a few personal disadvantages in the real world, like being a universal magnet for every instant entanglement and mismatched liaison on the planet. This explains that frequently frustrating social life with all the less-than-rewarding relationships or, as you see it, your inescapable fate, which it is until you make a conscious decision to bite that unavoidable bullet and begin the hard work of building your partnerships on the only foundation that can support them: mutual respect and total equality. You did make a promise to devote yourself to the hard work of creating equitable unions by balancing opposing forces, not manipulating them, which is why harmony and prosperity must now be achieved without losing yourself in the process, or worse, dominating whomever will let you. It's also why your happiness tends to head south whenever you try to either tyrannically control the important people in your life or just helplessly sacrifice yourself for the sake of keeping them in it. That's because surrendering to either one of these two self-serving behaviors is when a real partnership ceases to be one and, according to the cosmos, the real reason you're often without one.

Your Lazy Sun Syndrome Complaints: "My partners aren't devoted to me"; "My partners are always trying to control me."

Sun in the 8th House

With the Sun positioned in the 8th house of your natal chart, you have agreed to apply the hard-earned expertise of your Sun sign to the masterful management of mutual power. This means that you must now use your solar degree to transform yourself and others by skillfully controlling resources that just don't belong to you. Apparently, accessing your maximum potential not only depends on your ability to intuitively uncover any material, emotional, or psychological assets that are not your own, but on your ability to ingeniously manipulate them as well. As everyone knows, this can't be done without first achieving the deep level of intimacy that's needed to access them. You know, trust. No wonder you shine impressively whenever you direct your energies to the unknown complexities of financial management, research, and investigation, or life and death issues. With an 8th house Sun, you were born to dig below the surface, operate behind the scenes, and maneuver beneath the radar because you've been assigned to the difficult task of discovering our untapped reserves. This is primarily for the purpose of brilliantly controlling them, not emotionally manipulating us—but then, being at the top of your cosmic game is really just a matter of getting to the bottom of all aspects of life.

Because life itself usually begins with sex and ends with death, it's not hard to understand why you're so frequently exposed to the seamier side of humanity and so routinely involved with the more violent forces of nature. It's also why your own life gets a lot more complicated every time you're tempted to start unleashing what could be catastrophic or exposing what should be kept private just because you happened to be feeling threatened. After all, you promised to revolutionize our lives by dedicating your own to the wise use of hidden power, an assignment that just can't be accomplished without skillfully handling our property and cleverly keeping our secrets—not to mention eventually making a name for yourself, a fortune for others, and some powerful connections in the angst-ridden process. Understandably, that only occurs if you're clever enough to sidestep those typical 8th house land mines of bankrupt partners and legacy losses. Unfortunately, that never will occur until you're brave enough to step into our blood-curdling trenches and make the one thing you promised you would make: a difference.

Your Lazy Sun Syndrome Complaints: "No one else is as invested as I am"; "Everyone else has more resources than I do."

Sun in the 9th House

With the Sun positioned in the 9th house of your natal chart, you have agreed to apply the hard-earned expertise of your Sun sign to the physical pursuit of intellectual growth for the passionate purpose of universal enlightenment. This means that you must now use the power of your solar degree to broaden our mental awareness by expanding your earthly horizons. No wonder you can't help but shine heroically whenever you're challenging the limits of our intellectual, spiritual, and physical boundaries. You're the one who has been celestially selected to move beyond them. Evidently, your maximum potential can only be accessed by discovering the unknown opportunities and exploring the infinite possibilities that lie just outside the borders of your own childhood limitations and, it seems, our peripheral vision. The good news is that you're not without a cosmic compass on this lofty mission because the universe has blessed you with a noble sense of justice, a spirited sense of adventure, and an unobstructed view of the big picture. The not-so-good news is you'll need them.

With a 9th house Sun, you're not only committed to the intellectual responsibility of searching for knowledge and spreading the truth. You're pledged to the physical responsibility of defying the odds and going the distance to do so. This explains all those chronic crusades for justice and those compelling campaigns for the underdog, not to mention your undeniable talent when it comes to any far-reaching or advanced method of communication such as advertising, broadcasting, teaching, or publishing. You see, you were born to inspire the world as an outstanding example of your own deeply held convictions, which is why your opinionated path will always become strewn with overwhelming obstacles whenever you're not out there somewhere fearlessly preaching your principles and brilliantly voicing your views. Or worse, whenever you are out there anywhere, not practicing all of the beliefs and politics you so self-righteously advocate to us. Your soul did promise to become a powerful source of global enlightenment—a promise that can only be fulfilled through a continuous search for knowledge and the wise application of truth—yours. Luckily, this requires nothing more than leaving the so-called safety of your own intellectual backyard, and nothing less than taking us with you.

Your Lazy Sun Syndrome Complaints: "My rules must be followed"; "Their restrictions aren't necessary."

Sun in the 10th House

With the Sun positioned in the 10th house of your natal chart, you have agreed to apply the hard-earned expertise of your Sun sign to the ambitious pursuit of worldly success. This means that you must now use the powerful influence of your solar degree to become a powerful somebody in the outside world. Not to worry. With your political savvy, you know your powerful way around the inside track, which is ultimately a good thing because, officially, you're here to establish your place in society by rising to a position of authority. No wonder you're chronically compelled to impress the powers that be. You have a rendezvous with destiny to become one yourself, and you will, but only through the trials and tribulations of courageously calling the shots, respectfully running the show, and, oh yes, honorably following the rules, not manipulating them.

Accessing your maximum potential depends on your ability to demonstrate the responsible use of power, but not without first keeping your soul's promise to devote your earthly elbow grease to the hard work of earning it. That explains why the cosmos expects you to shine with supremacy when it comes to all aspects of parental authority, professional status, and public leadership. It also explains why every one of your occupational achievements is sure to be the result of your own father's recognition or, as is more often the cosmic case, motivated by the lack of it.

Either way, with your Sun committed to the global goldfish bowl of the 10th house, you'll find that you just can't avoid the spotlight of success whenever you're out there really trying to earn it. Nor, for that matter, can you escape the white-hot notoriety of public scrutiny whenever you're not trying. After all, you did come into a

THREE RIVERS PUBLIC LIBRARY
25207 W. CHANNON DRIVE
P.O. BOX 300
CHANNAHON, IL 60410-0300

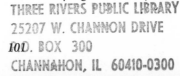

world that was universally prepared to expect great things of you, a world that, as far as you're concerned, seems to be constantly waiting for you to accomplish something, while never letting you get away with anything. That's because you were born at that time of day when the Sun was climbing to its highest point in the sky. A time when we only have to lift our eyes to see a brilliant star reach its most powerful peak. Evidently, the universe is expecting no less from you.

Your Lazy Sun Syndrome Complaints: "I never get the recognition I deserve"; "Why is everyone always in my business?"

Sun in the 11th House

With the Sun positioned in the 11th house of your natal chart, you have agreed to apply the hard-earned expertise of your Sun sign to the individual expression of social accomplishment. This means that you must now use the power of your solar degree to become an influential member of society by getting out there in the middle of humanity and asserting your own creative individuality. Sounds like a cosmic contradiction, doesn't it? Well, so does your 11th house mission. It's called group leadership, which is really nothing more than a planetary permission slip to openly pursue ambitious goals, eagerly embrace impossible dreams, and stubbornly support revolutionary ideas, while inspiring a group of otherwise ambivalent associates to follow your idealistic lead in the sometimes rebellious, but always progressive, process. Talk about ambitious goals.

Evidently, your maximum potential can only be reached by igniting our social awareness with your social conscience. No wonder you shine like a brilliant beacon of brotherhood whenever you're out there illuminating the issues and organizing the activities that are in some way crucial to the betterment of mankind, or at the very least, the local brownie troop. The fact is, you have the remarkable ability to do either one brilliantly because you have the vision and charisma to exhilarate everybody and, it seems, associate with anybody. This explains your impressive, yet unusual, buddy list of stimulating friends, powerful playmates, and justifiable weirdos. It also explains why you were born to endorse innovative people and embrace scientific principles. You're the one who is committed to a new and improved tomorrow, which, as far as you're concerned, requires devoting yourself to upsetting the status quo today. Unfortunately, according to the cosmos, this can only be achieved by demonstrating your individuality as an idealistic leader, not by arrogantly going your own willful way as an eccentric loner. Unless you prefer to stubbornly slip into those 11th house sinkholes of shattered hopes, domineering colleagues, and disappointing friendships. It's true you're expected to stand out as a member of society, but that's only because you've pledged yourself to the hard work of standing up for it. In fact, this lofty goal is very much like your own 11th house Sun. In order to be accomplished, it requires not only power and popularity, but the sobering realization that one can never be sacrificed for the other—and, of course, a little help from your friends.

Your Lazy Sun Syndrome Complaints: "The people I work with are too domineering"; "The groups I belong to are too ineffective."

Sun in the 12th House

With the Sun positioned in the 12th house of your natal chart, you have agreed to apply the hard-earned expertise of your Sun sign to the divine sacrifice of emotional service to others. This means that you must now use the power of your solar degree to universally elevate your own immortal spirit by compassionately rehabilitating ours. Talk about higher callings. Evidently, this is one lifetime that should come with a halo, not just because your soul is cosmically committed to providing others with the deep sense of emotional fulfillment they deserve, but because you're the one who must selflessly supply them with the strong sense of psychological well-being that they need. This is really no mortal task when you must first overcome your own childhood sense of guilt, loss, or shame before you do it. Is it any wonder that you're so influenced by the past?

With your Sun committed to the secrets, sorrows, and self-undoing of the 12th house, apparently you were born to heal it, and us. This is why you will always intuitively connect and indiscriminately merge with anything that appears to be familiar, seems to be suffering, or needs to be rescued. It's what you do, and why you shine with inspired results whenever we don't. That is, until you decide to use your wellspring of unlimited empathy and therapeutic special effects for something other than relieving our pain—like enabling it, or worse, escaping your own. That is usually when you stop impressing us as the brilliant power behind the throne and start annoying us as the neurotic martyr behind the scenes, while alienating us as you become your own worst enemy in the end. After all, your soul promised to use all that unconditional love, abstract awareness, and psychic insight to help us through our deepest fears and our darkest nights, not create them, and to awaken our spirit and brighten our tomorrows, not overwhelm them. It's really no coincidence that you were born just as the Sun was breaking over the eastern horizon and into our conscious awareness. This is the time of day when all human beings unconsciously accept enlightenment by instinctively opening their eyes to the brilliance of a higher power. Which, according to the cosmos, is supposed to be you.

Your Lazy Sun Syndrome complaints: "They have no right to keep secrets"; "I have every right to my privacy."

5

Saturn: Your Karmic Lesson

If all the year were playing holidays,
To sport would be as tedious as to work.

—WILLIAM SHAKESPEARE

Now don't let the mysterious rings and the turtle-like pace fool you, you're about to come face to face with the toughest planet in the solar system, which, not coincidentally, just happens to be the most demanding clause in your cosmic contract. This is Saturn, the astrological planet of responsibility, discipline, and limitation, or as it's officially referred to on the celestial circuit, the Taskmaster of the Universe. As every ancient astronomer could tell you, this is the planet that was purposely named after a ruthless, mythical giant who not only fathered gods, but also ate them when they misbehaved. That's why any decent astrologer will warn you that it's not the planet you want to mess with, at least not without a universal permission slip. There's a reason for that. According to universal law, Saturn was left in charge of your soul's growth, which means that, according to astrological lore, its position in the sky at the moment of your birth reflects how and where your soul made a promise to grow up in this lifetime.

Because that's a much easier promise for the spirit to make than it is for the flesh to keep, Saturn's position in the horoscope reveals just where you can expect to feel the crack of whatever particular cosmic whip it takes to make sure you do, and this means until you do. That's because while the cosmos did leave your soul with the personal responsibility of knowing what's good for you in this incarnation, it empowered Saturn with the universal purpose of seeing that you get it. Therefore, when it comes to the Saturn clause in your natal contract, you'd be wise not to expect anything you didn't work for, and even wiser to work for everything you actually do expect. Then again, when it comes to the Taskmaster, there's no excuse for anything less, only repercussions. There's also no real chance of avoiding either because, while Saturn may not be the most exciting planet in your chart or the most brilliant planet in the sky, in the vast cosmic scheme of things it does have more than just the daunting responsibility of making you more responsible. It has all the universal time, authority, and power it takes to actually make that happen.

What most of us tend to forget is that prior to the celestial debut of the telescope, Saturn was something other than just the sixth heavenly body from the Sun. In fact, until the end of the eighteenth century, it was more like the very last heavenly body in all of creation. In those myopic days of the Middle Ages, that's what it looked like to the first astronomers: the outermost planet on the cusp of the cosmos with an unthinkable 29½-year orbit around the Sun. While there's nothing outermost or unthinkable about Saturn today, these were the days when no one on earth could actually see beyond this planet, so it was scientifically safe to assume that nothing could possibly be beyond this planet. In an age when the average lifespan was not much longer than 30 years, who in their right medieval mind would ever believe that anything in the heavens could take almost as much time to get around the Sun as the average person could expect to spend living under it? Not many. Until, that is, our ancient astronomers peered into the cosmos and announced to the world that the sixth planet from the Sun was doing just that. Literally. It was actually circling the end of the universe in an orbit the length of a lifetime. According to their calculations, Saturn was not only up there working its weary, yet ambitious way around the Sun from the most remote location known to man and throughout the most severe conditions in the sky, it was somehow managing to do so with the reliability and precision of cosmic clockwork. No wonder they called it the "Taskmaster of the Universe." As far as these astronomers could actually see, this solar-deprived sphere was single-handedly keeping the cosmos together by holding down the difficult job of holding up the end of the universe.

That could mean only one thing to the ancient world. Saturn was nothing less than divine inspiration, which could mean only one other thing to everyone who was living on it. This godforsaken planet was not the most ill-fated member of the solar system after all. It was merely the most challenged. Despite what the medieval masses had come to believe, it wasn't up there inching through heaven on the brink of hell just because the weary world needed a poster-planet for all the hard work, hard luck, and hard times that lay ahead. Hardly. According to the best ancient minds, Saturn was out there in the middle of cosmic nowhere because people needed a universal example of how to overcome these things and an astronomical influence that was powerful enough to make sure we did. If our souls were ever going to grow up on this planet, then our bodies were going to have to succeed on it, and that meant we were going to have to get both the structure we needed to keep the cosmic promises we made, as well as the discipline we hated to overcome whatever it was that prevented us from keeping those promises in the past—accountability. This is not only where Saturn comes into the astrological picture, but why. This earthly journey of ours came with a couple of flawed human parents to keep our emotional, psychological, and physical development on track, but keeping our souls on task was going to require something a bit more enlightened and a lot less dysfunctional than the less than perfect role models that were biologically responsible for bringing us into the world. Our worldly success required having one universal authority to make sure the hard stuff went right; one that would always be ready to reflect the highest standards, enforce the strictest penalties, and uphold the tough restrictions; one that would force us to respect our universal boundaries, yet teach us to overcome our personal limitations. As planetary patriarch of the heavens, Saturn had only to demand from us here on earth what it was already practicing so brilliantly in the sky: responsible self-discipline.

What does Saturn mean in our individual natal chart? Exactly what it reflected in the medieval sky: limitations, hard work, and obstacles. It also represents what can be accomplished by overcoming them: success. If we're smart enough to read between the astrological rings, natal Saturn even reveals our own fail-safe universal formula for achieving it because the astrological sign Saturn occupied when we came into the world not only identifies how we acquired authority, assumed responsibility, and obtained respect yesterday, but where we were willing to work hard, play by the rules, and put in the time to get them. How? Well, to begin with, natal Saturn in:

Aries: Success and honor were earned through great physical disregard for danger and courageous acts of leadership in difficult times.

Taurus: Success and artistic status were earned by securing valuable assets and producing tangible results in times of deprivation.

Gemini: Success and academic authority were earned through the responsible delivery of news, people, and commodities in times of peril or hardship.

Cancer: Success and historical status were earned by protecting domestic stability, providing emotional nourishment, and preserving the past.

Leo: Success and glory were earned through the fearless display of leadership and brilliant creative achievements.

Virgo: Success and technical expertise were earned by diligently performing the routine tasks and services that were desperately needed by others.

Libra: Success and social status were earned by graciously creating beauty, attaining harmony, and establishing justice for those who had none.

Scorpio: Success and power were earned by masterfully demonstrating great emotional strength and resourcefulness in times of crisis or catastrophe.

Sagittarius: Success and prosperity were earned through noble acts of generosity, idealistic principles, and heroic defense of the underdog.

Capricorn: Success and professional honor were earned by demonstrating tremendous self-discipline, ambition, and integrity during times of great deprivation.

Aquarius: Success and freedom were earned through ingenious intellectual contributions to the betterment of humankind, science, and technology.

Pisces: Success and spiritual authority were earned through acts of tremendous physical sacrifices and great emotional service to others.

While it's always helpful to know just how you climbed the ladder of success in your last life, it's even more useful to learn just where that ladder can be found in this one. For that, we turn to our Saturn house, because in karmic astrology Saturn's placement in the natal chart is a universal reminder of where our status and authority waits for us in this life. Depressingly, however, that's only because Saturn's presence in the natal sky reflects our soul's karmic pledge to conquer whatever it was that kept us from achieving it in the last one. Evidently, Saturn can only predict our worldly accomplishment this time around because it actually reflects the very obstacle we must now overcome to achieve it. Conquer it we must then, no matter how difficult or insurmountable an obstacle it may be, because our Saturn house is that clause in our natal contract where we promised to pay for our success by working on ourselves. When we do, the cosmos is always quick to reward us with the status, authority, and success we deserve. It never fails. When we don't, Saturn is even quicker to remind us that real success is only achieved when human character has been strengthened. This is because the terms in our Saturn house are really quite simple: the only way for us to become a successful human being is by becoming a better one. According to the cosmos, that means overcoming the deep sense of fear or inadequacy that kept us from being successful in the first place. According to Saturn, this requires going into our Saturn house and physically facing something we lacked in the last life.

No wonder we all come into the world feeling so depressed or inadequate in the areas of life represented by our Saturn house. We are, but then if we weren't made to feel so desperately insufficient by our oldest failures, how else would we ever be motivated to work climb, and claw our way past them on to the success we could have been—the one the cosmos is waiting for us to be now. What better way to make sure we earn our own keep in the world than by giving us a place that makes us feel unworthy from the moment we come into it? Welcome to Saturn's house, the only place in the horoscope where our only goal is to grow up or die trying. Well, maybe we won't really die from any of the crippling insecurities or heavy responsibilities that we're forced to shoulder in these dreary digs, but there will be times when we're convinced we will, or wish we could. This is where Saturn does what he must to make sure we suffer through more than our fair share of severe punishments, dismal restrictions, and, for some sadistic reason, the painful inadequacies of our own human father as well.

We should not be surprised. This is the house where we can't help but be deeply affected by the first authority figures in our lives, or at least our perception of them, because this is where we made an appointment with the universe to become one ourselves. Our

Saturn house is where our patience and ambition must now be applied because this is where our soul promised the cosmos that we would earn our own authority in this life. As a result, our Saturn house is where even the smallest goal or slightest success will always require a good deal of doing without and a great deal of doing it all, not to mention a whole lot of doing the time. In fact, in most cases, nothing less than 29 ½ years. Why? Because in every case, we're cosmically required to spend at least as much time as it takes Saturn to make one orbit around the Sun, learning that real authority is never acquired without responsibility, and true success is never achieved without effort, and, in every horoscope, we're required to learn it here, not just because acing this class is our only way up in the material world, but because, more importantly, it's our soul's only way out of it. While practical astrology teaches us that our Saturn lesson is always learned after our first Saturn return at the age of 29 ½, through karmic astrology we realize that Saturn's lesson can't be learned until then because that's how much time we're required to spend learning it. That is why some people don't get the success or status they signed up for until after the age of 45 to 50, and worse, some people don't get it at all. Fortunately, we don't have to be one of them if we only get this: Natal Saturn is your 29 ½-year karmic lesson, and the house it occupies in your birth chart is your karmic classroom.

While getting through our own particular lesson plan in our own particular Saturn house is no romp in the astrological park, that's because it's more than just the best way to become the somebody we said we'd be in this lifetime. It's the only way to become the higher soul we're supposed to be in the next one—the same way the most star-crossed chunk of universal real estate in the heavens ended up becoming the most powerful symbol of authority in the birth chart—the hard way, the disciplined way. We do know now that Saturn was never the last stop in the universe, as the ancient world thought it was. What we didn't know then is that it was always something much more significant—the first universal success story, the one that came from behind and got to the top by doing its best in spite of the worst. In fact, it's for that very reason that, to this very day, Saturn is still the only astrological influence that brings discipline into our lives. A long time ago, when we needed it most, Saturn was the first universal energy to bring boundaries into our consciousness.

Saturn in the 1st House

Your soul's karmic lesson in this lifetime is physical independence, which means your crippling insecurities, heavy responsibilities, and severe limitations will always be experienced in those areas of life that are fundamental to personal development: your early childhood, your physical body, and your self-esteem.

For this reason, you were inflicted with some type of childhood limitation that was physically confining, such as a difficult birth, a congenital disability, or a restricted upbringing. What better way to get you into such a depressing karmic classroom, which brings us to why you were instilled with all those deep feelings of inadequacy about who you are and what you're never going to be in the first place. Personal humiliation is your only incentive for getting out. Getting out is never going to happen until you start getting busy on yourself. According to the cosmos, before you can achieve the total physical independence you signed up for, you must first spend about 29½ years earning it. Nothing less, because according to Saturn, that's about how long it's going to take to develop the disciplined ego, the responsible self-sufficiency, and the grown-up reliability that real independence requires. Identifying your biggest fears and then bravely conquering the worst of them is something that can't be accomplished overnight—only over time, and only by yourself. In fact, the personal freedom and physical success you long for will never become a reality until you can demonstrate to the universe that your self-loathing no longer is. Fortunately, there is an upside to this 1st house Saturn. It not only brings great staying power to every physical effort you make, it brings an increase in personal status almost every time you do, which means that if anyone has what it takes to single-handedly annihilate both their toughest challenge and their biggest obstacle, it's you. Unfortunately, the downside of a 1st house Saturn is that, quite often, your toughest challenge and biggest obstacle actually is you.

Saturn in the 2nd House

Your soul's karmic lesson in this lifetime is material security, which means your crippling inadequacies, heavy responsibilities, and severe limitations will always be experienced in those areas of life that are fundamental to acquiring anything of tangible value. In general, this would be the personal income, material possessions, and financial resources areas of life—in particular, your personal net worth.

No wonder you were forced to endure some type of severe economic anxiety early on in life, such as an upbringing that failed to meet your basic needs or a childhood where authority figures just couldn't provide for you. Material deprivation is how Saturn got you into this karmic classroom, and burdening you with a deep sense of financial insecurity is how Saturn plans on getting you out. There's really no better motivation for achieving material success than being instilled with an unrealistic fear of poverty, and, according to the cosmos, no more important lesson for you to learn than that the worth of what you own is determined by the strength of what you value. That is why this 2nd house Saturn made you do without the big stuff you needed back then. You were being taught to look within for the real stuff that mattered right now, the stuff worth having. For that you must first develop a reliable value system and use it, because, until the cosmos is convinced that ethical earnings and charitable spending is actually your standard way of living, physical comfort and material satisfaction won't be. If your money flows out in a responsible, generous, and disciplined manner, Saturn will always make sure it flows back when you need it, sometimes even miraculously. With natal Saturn running things in your "valuable stuff" house, it's no secret that you're actually destined to someday have every material thing your heart desires. It won't be before you're 29½ though, because it can't be until after you've earned for yourself the one personal thing money can't buy: self-worth.

Saturn in the 3rd House

Your soul's karmic lesson in this lifetime is intellectual development, which means your crippling insecurities, heavy responsibilities, and severe limitations will always be experienced in those areas of life that are fundamental to the immediate learning environment. In general, this would be the primary education, neighborhood community, and local relatives areas of life—in particular, your social networks.

This is exactly why you experienced such great difficulty learning when you were younger and also why you had to put up with those not-so-great educational opportunities when you were a little older. This is the karmic classroom of restricted education, the Saturn house, where some type of learning disability, scholastic disadvantage, or language deficiency is the iron-clad requirement for getting in. The deep feelings of intellectual inadequacy that accompany them are your foolproof incentive for getting out. Not to worry. This 3rd house Saturn made sure you had plenty of both, which explains why you often felt like an intellectual outsider in your own family, classroom, and neighborhood when you were a child. How else could you be expected to build the reliable networks you needed and develop the responsible communication skills you signed up for if siblings weren't somehow making you feel lonely, classmates weren't sometimes making you feel stupid, and neighbors weren't somewhere putting up fences. You couldn't, which is why they did, and why you must now roll up your intellectual sleeves and connect yourself to the community by becoming the most reliable source of accurate information, dependability, and practical ideas in it.

According to the cosmos, you'll never achieve the worldly success you seek until after you've earned the intellectual authority you never had. This, according to Saturn, can't be achieved without first spending at least 29 ½ years developing the mental discipline and social maturity that a task like that requires. Apparently, you'll never stop being challenged by words or intimidated by information until this Saturn is convinced that you can deliver both to the community responsibly.

Saturn in the 4th House

Your soul's karmic lesson in this lifetime is domestic stability, which means your crippling insecurities, heavy responsibilities, and severe limitations will always be experienced in those areas of life that are fundamental to achieving emotional security. In general, this would be your family, domestic scene, and native country areas of life. In particular, this is the nurturing you received as a child, your mother, and your early home life.

Not surprisingly then, your early home life was either emotionally deprived or severely restricted by a parent who was in some way psychologically punishing, emotionally unavailable, or confined to the home due to age, hardship, or disease. Welcome to the karmic classroom of emotional insecurity—the original "home alone" house where inadequate nurturing is Saturn's only requirement for getting in. That's because the deep fear of emotional rejection you picked up at the door is your only motivation for getting out. No wonder you grew up without feeling any unconditional love or approval inside your home. You were being taught how to obtain the maternal acceptance you needed from someplace inside yourself—and you can—but only by unlearning all the critical, strict, and inflexible emotional responses that were taught to you as a child, and only by forgiving the critical, strict, and inflexible caregivers who taught them to you. This happens somewhere around the age of 29½ because that's usually when the less-than-perfect people who raised you suddenly realize that you can take care of yourself.

Unfortunately, it's also when you suddenly realize that you must take care of them. In this house parents become burdens, because in this house Saturn not only insists that you become your own source of emotional nourishment, it demands that you show compassion for the inadequate tribe members who came before you. In fact, according to the cosmos, you're destined to successfully establish the loving home and nurturing family you never had as a child. With Saturn in the building, however, it won't be without first tearing down the resentful walls you put up as an adult.

Saturn in the 5th House

Your soul's karmic lesson in this lifetime is personal distinction, which means your crippling insecurities, heavy responsibilities, and severe limitations will always be experienced in those areas of life that are fundamental to any kind of individual self-expression. In general, this would be the joyful, artistic, and creative areas of life. In particular, that means your creations, your passions, and your children.

That explains why you experienced a childhood in which your self-esteem was severely bruised, your creative talent was greatly inhibited, or your fun and happiness was extremely limited. This is the karmic classroom of killjoy parenting. The Saturn house where being made to feel insignificant or unworthy in your formative years is the only criteria for getting in, and that life-long inferiority complex that comes with it is your only incentive for getting out. But then there's really no better motivation for achieving the personal honor and glory you signed up for than believing that you have yet to become the great source of pride and joy that your parents had hoped for. No wonder all that unconditional love, attention, and applause you deserved seemed so depressingly hard to come by back then. You were being taught how to recognize your own star power when your mother wouldn't, celebrate your own artistic brilliance when your father couldn't, and generate your own zest for life when the adult world didn't. That means you were being forced to apply your talent toward the very one thing a joyful artist requires and this 5th house Saturn demands—a powerful sense of self—and you must, because until you do, life won't sparkle, love won't sizzle, and creations won't dazzle, including your children. But then, how could they? According to the cosmos, personal distinction is only achieved by putting your fragile ego out on a creative limb and courageously demonstrating passion, and, while this Saturn is willing to give you 29½-years to learn how to take an emotional chance in life, it won't give you center stage until you can take a creative risk on yourself.

Saturn in the 6th House

Your soul's karmic lesson in this lifetime is physical productivity, which means your crippling insecurities, heavy responsibilities, and severe limitations will always be experienced in those areas of life that are fundamental to the efficiency of your physical work, health, and fitness. In particular, this would be the everyday tasks, routine activities, and physical exercise areas of life—in general, your daily grind.

No wonder you were forced to endure the childhood humiliation of either a hard-to-please parent, a critical upbringing, or an argumentative household. This is the karmic classroom of physical incompetence and intellectual inadequacy—the Saturn house of self-proclaimed doormats—where being made to feel incapable of doing anything right is the only way in, and where being instilled with an irrational sense of responsibility for fixing everything wrong is the only way out. There's really no better motivation for developing the necessary skills to improve the quality of our daily lives than being burdened by an overwhelming sense of duty early on, in yours. That's what a 6th house Saturn does. It's also the reason you were the one who always seemed to have more work, more worry, and more restrictions than anyone else when you were younger. You were being taught how to be of practical service to everyone else when you were older, which won't be before the age of 29 ½ because, according to Saturn, it can't be until you've actually acquired the technical knowledge or developed the specialized skills that are somehow critical to making our world more efficient and yours more rewarding.

With a 6th house Saturn, your success depends not just on your ability to stop complaining about the high degree of excellence that others expect of you, but on your willingness to start making whatever physical sacrifices are necessary to give it to them. Until you do, good jobs will be hard to find, good employees will be hard to keep, and good health will be hard to come by. You'll never be successful until this Saturn is convinced you're being useful.

Saturn in the 7th House

Your soul's karmic lesson in this lifetime is mutual commitment, which means your crippling insecurities, heavy responsibilities, and severe limitations will always be experienced in those areas of life that are fundamental to establishing important one-on-one relationships. In general, that would be the marriage, partnership, and contractual agreements areas of life—in particular, your significant others.

That is the real reason that your relationship with authority figures, in general, and your own father, in particular, was in some way restricted, lacking, or incomplete when you were a child. It's also why you now go through life always seeking that "parent" when establishing what's supposed to be your coequal relationships as an adult. This is the karmic classroom of "make room for daddy," the Saturn house where having unfinished business with paternal figures is the only prerequisite for getting in, and that profound feeling of being unable to relate to others because of it is the only incentive for getting out. According to the cosmos, the best motivation for successfully connecting to the people who matter today is the feeling of being so disconnected from those who mattered the most yesterday. It's also the reason your first relationships with authority figures left you feeling insecure and unfulfilled when you were younger. This 7th house Saturn was teaching you how to accept responsibility for making your primary relationships more successful when you were older by making them more reciprocal.

This is a lesson that can't be taught in less than 29½ years because, according to Saturn, it can't be learned without developing the collaborative skills and the responsible backbone that real commitment demands and all grown-ups require. That means that until you stop giving up power and start looking for equals, partners will be burdens, relationships will be lacking, and you'll be alone. With the taskmaster cracking his whip in your "significant others house," you're actually destined to achieve success through powerful mergers with responsible grown-ups—unfortunately, not without becoming one first.

Saturn in the 8th House

Your soul's karmic lesson in this lifetime is the intense sharing of life-changing resources, which means your crippling insecurities, heavy responsibilities, and severe limitations will always be experienced in those areas of life that are fundamental to accessing the financial, emotional, or psychological reserves of others. In general, this would be the intimate and meaningful areas of life. In particular, that means the financial assets, sexual desires, powerful secrets, or life-and-death experiences you share with others.

For that reason you were forced to experience some type of parental conditioning when you were a child that either restricted your ability to demonstrate raw emotion, inhibited your capacity to express unrestrained passion, or caused you to become unduly obsessed with controlling your own appetites and desires. This is survival Saturn style, the karmic classroom where a childhood lack of material resources is the only criteria for getting in, because the deep feeling of inadequacy that comes from being at the financial mercy of others is your only incentive for getting out.

No wonder you were made to feel so dependent on the power of others just to get along in life. You had to learn how to create what you needed to access the even bigger powers later on in life, trust—which brings us to the real lesson being taught in this house, intimacy—and the real work that you and your soul signed up for, getting past the emotional blockage of yesterday and learning to trust in yourself today. This, according to the cosmos, can't be achieved without first demonstrating your complete trust in the power of your own instincts and desires now, not by either stoically denying them or hedonistically indulging in them, but by using them to responsibly fuel your purpose and, ultimately, your success. So get busy, because this 8th house Saturn isn't going to let you tap into any other source of power until you've spent at least 29½ years and a few gut-wrenching moments proving to the rest of the world that you know how to use your own.

Saturn in the 9th House

Your soul's karmic lesson in this lifetime is intellectual growth, which means your crippling insecurities, heavy responsibilities, and severe limitations will always be experienced in those areas of life that are fundamental to your spiritual enlightenment. In general, this would be the advanced learning, higher philosophy, and long-distance experience areas of life—in particular, your educational adventures.

Is it any wonder then that your early development was either intellectually stunted or physically restricted by the fanatical beliefs, conservative policies, or intolerant attitudes of a dominant parental influence? It shouldn't be. This is the karmic classroom of "obstructed horizons," the Saturn house where being overwhelmed by the intellectual, spiritual, or physical limitations of a dreary childhood is your lonely ticket in, and being even more overwhelmed by the fear that you're just not smart enough to move beyond them is your only ticket out.

That explains all the rigid traditions and ruthless opinions that inhibited your learning as a child. You were being forced to look elsewhere for the answers you wanted and the education you needed as an adult, someplace far beyond the physical limits and mental boundaries of your childhood upbringing. Far away is not only where your higher education really lies, it's where your earthly success is guaranteed.

While neither is likely until you've spent at least 29 ½ years proving to this Saturn that you're much more adventurous and far less judgmental than your parents, that's usually how long it takes for you to be dragged kicking and screaming over that dreaded horizon to your very first elsewhere. You'd be wise to go, because until you stop looking for knowledge in all the wrong places and start dishing out truth that isn't self-righteous, you'll never be as well traveled as you could be or as well-schooled as you should be. You'll never learn how to stop intimidating the world with what you know and start enlightening it—which, according to Saturn, is not only how you actually become wise but when you finally grow up.

Saturn in the 10th House

Your soul's karmic lesson in this lifetime is worldly success, which means your crippling insecurities, heavy burdens, and severe limitations will always be experienced in those areas of life that are fundamental to achieving any kind of official responsibility. In general, this would be the professional career and public achievements areas of life. In particular, that means your father, other figures of authority, and the outside world.

That is why you grew up never getting the undivided attention you always wanted from your father, the emotional validation you genuinely needed from your parents, or the standing ovation you obviously deserved from the adult world. This is the karmic classroom of "too many rules and too little praise," the Saturn house where being raised by what you believed was a very cold parent in a really cruel world is the only requirement for getting in. Being motivated by an irrational fear of social judgment, or worse, public failure, is the only incentive for getting out or, in your case, getting to the top.

That brings us to why you were forced to grow up without knowing your own father's influence or affection as a child. According to the cosmos, you had to learn how to publicly succeed in life by somehow mastering the cold, cruel world without them. This, according to Saturn, can only be achieved by spending the first 29½ years of it developing the moral integrity and responsible work ethic that real success requires, not the ruthless tactics and cutthroat policies that blind ambition fosters. Therefore, unless this Saturn is convinced you're out there putting in the time, playing by the rules, and working up a sweat, you won't be getting the credit you deserve for anything—only the blame you don't deserve for everything. But then you're not supposed to achieve professional success in spite of the heartless parenting and unforgiving world you had to endure as a child. With a 10th house Saturn, when you finally rise to that honorable position of authority, it will actually be because of them.

Saturn in the 11th House

Your soul's karmic lesson in this lifetime is social contribution, which means your crippling insecurities, heavy responsibilities, and severe limitations will always be experienced in those areas of life that are fundamental to collective accomplishment. In general, this would be the idealistic visions, group affiliations, and social participation areas of life—in particular, your friends, peers, and associates.

It's not hard to understand why you grew up with either too much parental emphasis on discipline, respect, and following the rules; too few childhood opportunities for rebellion, freedom, and nonconformity; or too many dominant authority figures involved in your upbringing. This is the karmic classroom of "odd man out," the Saturn house where being conventionally raised by a parent who was older, stricter, or squarer than any of the others you knew is the only requirement for getting in. Never being able to feel completely comfortable in large groups of people your own age is Saturn's 11th house inadequacy for getting out. How else could you ever be expected to develop the social skills and humanitarian ideals you signed up for if colleagues weren't always so domineering, teammates weren't always so disapproving, and friendships weren't always so disappointing? You couldn't, which is why this Saturn made sure they were, and why you must now come together with large groups of different people to pool your creative energies and inspire each other's vision, even the weird and inferior ones.

It's your karmic responsibility to make a more powerful contribution to society than one person is capable of making by themselves, which means it's now your karmic lesson to learn how to effectively work, dream, and play with your peers, especially the weird and inferior ones. Despite what you grew up believing, conforming to the standards of society isn't what keeps your parents' approval or the sky from falling—participating in it is, and that, according to Saturn, takes a good 29 ½ years of not looking down your nose at it.

Saturn in the 12th House

Your soul's karmic lesson in this lifetime is emotional wholeness, which means your crippling insecurities, heavy responsibilities, and severe limitations will always be experienced in those areas of life that are fundamental to healing the unconscious past. In general, this would be the psychological strength, emotional health, and eternal soul areas of life—in particular, your spiritual life.

This is why you were forced to cope with some type of profound loss or emotional sacrifice in your formative years, such as a father who faded from your life at an early age, a rejecting parent who failed to respond to your basic emotional needs, or an unhealthy upbringing that lacked the authority, stability, or protection you needed to feel safe. This is the karmic classroom of "childhood lost," the Saturn house where being made to feel either physically, mentally, or emotionally abandoned when you were younger is the mandatory burden of hopelessness for getting in. Being instilled with a profound sense of guilt and unworthiness because of it is the only real hope you have of ever getting out.

There's really no better motivation for seeking to become part of something that is greater than yourself and committed to a higher cause than harboring an irrational belief that you'll only be left alone to fend for yourself by anyone lesser who isn't. No wonder your emotional suffering was necessary back then. This Saturn was teaching you how to develop the unconditional faith, creative imagination, and psychological strength you needed to achieve your divine objective today: forgiveness. With a 12th house Saturn, it's now your karmic responsibility to provide compassion to those people who need it the most. This, according to the cosmos, is really just a matter of forgiving all the people that you think deserve it the least. So let go of them and your past, because even though you and your soul are destined to bask in the glory of spiritual success for the rest of eternity, it won't be before you've spent at least 29½ years on this planet earning it.

6

Neptune: Your Karmic Debt

Upon such sacrifices, my Cordelia,
The gods themselves throw incense.

—WILLIAM SHAKESPEARE

Prepare yourself. As the astrological planet of faith, spirituality, mystery, and illusion, Neptune is, without question, the thorn in your cosmic contract. That's because, as the universal ruler of your unconscious soul, it was meant to be the angst of your earthly existence.

In fact, just getting a glimpse of the eighth planet in our solar system is no cosmic piece of cake, as there are few objects more difficult to locate in the night sky than this mysterious sphere of isolated beauty. Nevertheless, once our telescopes manage to do that, few are more fascinating. In fact, the first astronomers to physically observe Neptune in the mid-nineteenth-century heavens perceived it to be a very compelling, ever evasive, truly inspiring, and yet highly deceptive influence in the universe. Not surprisingly, that is the very same impact they determined it to have in the horoscope. From its very first orbit into our awareness, Neptune has always managed to emerge on the scene, and through the lens, as nothing less than a faraway world seductively beckoning from the enchanting serenity of another dimension—its own—or what today's astrologers would call the twilight zone. Yesterday's astrologers were right, Neptune is deceiving. With a cosmic zip code thirty times farther from the Sun than ours and an impossibly frigid atmosphere of liquid, clouds, and gases, this planet's ethereal appearance is really nothing more than just an icy illusion of its own heavily veiled environment, an environment so thick with methane that it not only sparks treacherous storms and spawns poisonous winds, but cleverly conceals their existence under a beautiful blanket of blue-green vapor.

So much for appearances, not to mention our grasp on reality. Evidently, the very essence of this dark and inhabitable planet personifies the most basic of human conditions: when faced with intolerable circumstances, people tend to see what they want to see. This is exactly why we continuously overlook Neptune's influence in the sky and consistently underestimate its significance at our birth. This planet is never what it appears to be, either in the heavens or the horoscope.

But then, according to yesterday's stargazers, how could it be? From a universal perspective, they determined Neptune to be nothing less than the mirror of our soul, which means from an astrological one, it's nothing more than a celestial shadow of our unconscious past, our creative imagination, and our unconditional faith—guilt and addictions included. Because Neptune's presence in the natal sky reflects our soul's longing to become its glorious best, Neptune's placement in the natal chart reveals the particular wrong that we must right down here on terra firma in order to redeem our torturous past. As the mirror of our soul, it is Neptune's primary purpose to remind us of our previous fall from grace by dutifully and perpetually reflecting it back to us. This is usually when things get kind of messy for us because, with Neptune as the universal projector, this painful human wrongdoing tends to look more to us like a paid vacation in the Bahamas than the earthly obligation it really is. That's when the real torture begins, because if there's anything we need to address in this life with our eyes wide open, it's exactly what this planet represents in the natal chart: our very own karmic debt to the universe, or, as it's more commonly known, our soul's previous agreement to emotionally replace, in this lifetime, what it selfishly depleted in the last one.

Here you are and you know the story: once upon a time, after the big bang, but before we came into this incarnation, our soul signed up for another earthly lifetime of physical growth and intellectual development—this one—which is when the soul and the cosmos got together and collectively agreed upon a very specific type of universal community service that would have to be performed in this lifetime in order to compensate for a very specific act of personal selfish gain that we committed in a previous one. Because our unconscious soul is the part of us that made this karmic agreement back then, we have no conscious memory of it today, which is why we tend to spend the better part of our human lives antagonizing the universe by making no attempt to keep it. In an effort to remind us of this outstanding emotional debt, the universe calls on the highly creative and somewhat questionable tactics of Neptune to remind us, and because these tactics are so questionable, we just ignore them, which is when they just become more creative and we fall victim to them.

Obviously, our spiritual payback would be a whole lot less torturous if we weren't all so willing to abandon the harsh realities of planet earth for those appealing, yet toxic, illusions of the twilight zone. Instead of heeding Neptune's perpetual calls to heal the painful undoings of our past, we're often woefully enticed to spin our wistful wheels revisiting them. Then we're somehow genuinely shocked to find ourselves reliving it, which is exactly how this planet manages to inspire us on to the unlimited joy of our higher calling one minute and lure us back into the emotional despair of our once-upon-a-time the next. We should know better, you can't go home again, right? Wrong. Unlike any other place in the cosmos, Neptune is the one place where we can go home again. In fact, because Neptune is home to the soul, it's the only place in the cosmos where going home is effortless, and that's why it's hell for us. What most of us have yet to understand is that in this contractual agreement called our birth chart, Neptune is not a painful experience we're supposed to revisit. It's an emotional scale we agreed to balance in this lifetime and without the help of any blue-green vapor.

Wouldn't it be a lot easier to just roll up our spiritual sleeves and perform whatever philanthropic feat the universe expects of us? Naturally. As far as our karmic debt is concerned, that's half the battle—the second half. The first half is remembering that we have an outstanding obligation to begin with, and determining what that is. For this we turn to our natal Neptune. To begin with, the astrological sign Neptune occupied at the moment of our birth is a universal acknowledgment of how we earned our spiritual stripes in our most previous lifetime. This sign reflects the karmic skills we've been blessed with today because it mirrors the great personal sacrifice we made somewhere along that joyless journey of yesterday. For instance, natal Neptune in:

Virgo: Reflects a dedicated perfectionist whose compassion was demonstrated by efficiently performing the routine but thankless tasks that were critically needed by others.

Libra: Reflects a talented peacemaker who brought joy and happiness to those who had none by creating beauty, achieving harmony, and establishing justice where it was lacking.

Scorpio: Reflects a masterful manipulator whose compassion for the weak was powerfully displayed through the wise use of shared resources in times of great crisis or catastrophe.

Sagittarius: Reflects an idealistic hero whose strong morals and deeply held convictions were generously used to support the needy and defend the underdog when no one else would.

Capricorn: Reflects a powerful public figure whose professional status, office, or power was used to honorably influence and oversee the orphaned or underprivileged.

Aquarius: Reflects a brilliant humanitarian who supported the poor and forgotten outcasts of society by establishing brotherhood, developing new forms of energy, or advancing technology.

Pisces: Reflects an enlightened healer whose divine faith, compassion, and imagination were used to emotionally comfort the hopeless and psychologically heal the helpless.

While our Neptune sign is an insightful peek at the past, our Neptune house is the cosmic key to our future. Its placement in the natal chart identifies the specific area of life where the universe expects us to sacrifice our self-interest in the present because its location in the natal sky documents where our soul promised to redeem the self-serving sins of our past. This can only be achieved by compassionately and unselfishly providing to those who are needier than us a little bit of whatever it is our own Neptune house represents. Could payback be any easier than this? Doesn't that mean we only have to write a generous check to our favorite Neptune house charity or hold the door for the poor guy with crutches in that particular part of our lives and, abracadabra, our universal debt is paid in full? Not really. The truth is that while ignoring Neptune's call to service is nothing short of emotional suicide, balancing this outstanding debt requires nothing less than emotional sacrifice. For that reason, by universal design, we're actually scheduled to experience some type of early loss or childhood misery in our Neptune house—a universal memo, if you will, to remind us of our soul's promise by making us painfully aware and therefore intimately connected to the very same suffering we've agreed to lessen for others.

In theory, this really is quite a good plan, but, as we humans seem hell-bent on proving, not an infallible one, primarily because it's often a confusing one. Neptune is the planet of faith and imagination, which means that we're just as gifted when it comes to this particular planet as we are encumbered. Therefore, although our Neptune house is definitely the area of life where we've been burdened with emotional hardship, it's also exactly where we've been blessed with enough inspiration and creativity to overcome it, and, for reasons we have yet to understand, the same place where we never seem to be consciously aware of either. Obviously, the universe not only expects to be cosmically compensated in this area of the natal chart, it expects us to do so by using our Neptune energies to create the unimaginable, believe the incredible, and realize the impossible. Unfortunately, when we choose to do less, this is exactly where the universe magnanimously settles for a more human method of payment: our blood, sweat, and tears.

This, as any stargazer will tell you, is only made possible through what is astrologically known as the Neptune nudge, but more humanly experienced as something a little less ethereal. Most of us know it as that irresistible force we often come up against that somehow always manages to propel us into that overwhelming event we didn't anticipate, while never failing to provide us with an unbearably unobstructed view of profound suffering—in most cases, our own. Not surprisingly, this is usually when we become inspired to develop a less agonizing method for dealing with that kind of pain than the unpleasant practice of acknowledging it, like perhaps altering the way we perceive it. That happens to be something we do rather well in our Neptune house, because that happens to be the one place in our lives where we've been instilled with enough inspired vision to make anything look more appealing by just skillfully surrounding it with our own blue-green cloud cover of escapism, denial, or addiction. If, that is, we haven't already unconsciously fallen victim to the power of someone else's vision. No wonder secrets, scandal, drugs, and all things illegal have little difficulty making their wicked way into our lives through the door of Neptune's domain. In fact, because this is the house where we've been equipped to believe the unimaginable and hope for the best, it's also where we're now most likely to be deceived by the lies and delusions of others. It's also where we're least likely to recognize our own.

If Neptune is beginning to sound like our celestial shot at sainthood, that's only because it is. In fact, its placement in the natal chart is the only spot in the universe where we are both armed and authorized to achieve the impossible, but, as Neptune is so quick to remind us, never by avoiding the inevitable. No other house in the natal chart guarantees our spiritual reward because no other universal energy compels our emotional sacrifice. Our Sun house requires our complete personal commitment because it promises our inevitable superstardom, and our Saturn house insists that we conquer our human fears and obstacles because it demands that we earn our earthly success. But our Neptune house, for no apparent reason, expects us to give until it hurts, or else, as the cosmos assures us, it will. If we don't, it usually does. When we do, that's when we understand the true meaning of being our glorious best, but only by recognizing our Neptune house for what it really is—our earthly tour of emotional duty.

While it's never the tropical island getaway we would like it to be, it only becomes an emotional prison when we choose to pretend otherwise or decide to ignore it altogether, making life in our Neptune house really quite simple. This is where we must balance our debt and experience the joy of the best-is-yet-to-come, or ignore our commitment and wallow in the sorrow of here-we-go-again. With Neptune on the scene, it's also one of the only two places in the natal chart where we always seem to have great difficulty telling the difference between the two (Neptune's home, the 12th house, is the other), and because of that, the only reason Neptune never fails to pull out the hardware and start polishing up the nudges when we can't. In the long human haul, that may not be such a bad thing, especially if it gets us to fulfill our karmic obligation and, by doing so, our destiny. That's because the real key to understanding natal Neptune is nothing more than coming to the realization that our universal obligation is our personal destiny. It's that simple. We must provide others willingly with the emotional support that's required of us, or be prepared to have it taken from us arbitrarily. We must assist those who are lost and less fortunate in our Neptune area of life, or just completely ignore their pain and deprivation—until, of course, we get nudged, and then it becomes ours. Ultimately, Neptune's promise of enlightenment can't be avoided because neither can our debt. Either we balance our karmic scale with the inspiration, empathy, and mercy we promised or writhe with remorse when Neptune comes looking for our blood, sweat, and tears. The choice, like the toxic illusion, is entirely up to us. We can serve compassionately or we can suffer emotionally. Either way, the universe gets paid.

Neptune in the 1st House

Universal Payback: You

With natal Neptune placed in the 1st house of "Me, Myself, and I," this karmic debt appears to be the result of a previous lifetime in which you chose to gratify your ego through either violent abuse or reckless neglect of personal independence, personal ambition, or physical action. In some willful way, your angry, headstrong, or aggressive behavior allowed you to impulsively deprive others of developing their own self-confidence while you egotistically dominated them with yours. No wonder the guilt from yesterday's gung ho involvement inspires today's lazy indifference. Although frequently compelled by your own highly developed physical response to music, art, harmony, and rhythm, your karmic payback in the here and now requires your unselfish service as a positive influence on the physical talents and abilities that foster self-esteem in others. If not, expect a painful loss in the areas of life that contribute to your own.

In particular, your birth, identity, title, personality, personal independence, personal actions, physical body, physical appearance, early childhood.

Neptune in the 2nd House

Universal Payback: Your Stuff

With natal Neptune placed in the 2nd house of "What's Mine is Mine," this karmic debt appears to be the result of a previous lifetime in which the tangible benefits of personal values, sensual pleasure, and material prosperity were either improperly embraced or carelessly neglected. In one materialistic way or another, your wasteful, greedy, or negligent handling of precious resources and personal possessions deprived others of the financial rewards they deserved or the physical comforts they needed. No wonder today's money slips so easily through yesterday's guilty fingers. Although frequently compelled by your intuitive ability to recognize and appreciate value, your karmic payback in the here and now requires your unselfish service in helping others acquire the material self-worth they so desperately need. If not, expect a painful loss through the areas of life that contribute to your own.

In particular, your personal value system, earning skills, earning power, money, stocks/bonds, financial affairs, bank accounts, moveable possessions, material resources, tangible assets.

Neptune in the 3rd House

Universal Payback: Your Network

With natal Neptune placed in the 3rd house of your "local landscape," this karmic debt appears to be the result of a previous lifetime in which your responsibility for local communications, education, commerce, or transportation was fraudulently abused or carelessly neglected. Neighborhood friends, relatives, and classmates suffered greatly when you permitted ideas to be exchanged, news to be circulated, or individuals to be moved with a lack of concern for the details or a reckless disregard for the community. No wonder today's siblings and neighbors can easily rekindle yesterday's guilt. Although you are frequently compelled by your highly developed, yet often confusing, intuition, your karmic payback in the here and now requires your unselfish service in the responsible networking of people, merchandise, and information within the intellectual neighborhood. If not, expect a painful loss through the areas of life that define your own.

In particular, your experiences with siblings, neighbors, classmates, close-by relatives, communications, schools, learning ability, education, merchandising transactions, vehicles, local transportation.

Neptune in the 4th House

Universal Payback: Your Family Nest

With natal Neptune placed in the 4th house of "Home Sweet Home," this karmic debt appears to be the result of a previous lifetime in which the emotional sanctuaries of home, family, maternal care, or the ancestral past were resentfully abused or carelessly neglected. Unable to live up to your lofty ideals, your own family, children, parents, or country were not only disgraced by the depth of your disappointment, but disabled by the shame of their own insufficiency. No wonder yesterday's guilty secret can still be found in today's family closet. Although frequently overwhelmed by strong psychic feelings and bouts of maudlin sentimentality, your karmic payback in the here and now requires your unselfish service in providing others with the emotional nourishment or domestic security they so desperately need. If not, expect a painful loss in the areas of life that contribute to your own.

In particular, experiences with family, mother, nurturing ability, home, land, real-estate, agriculture, ancestry, culture, homeland/country.

Neptune in the 5th House

Universal Payback: Your Creations

With natal Neptune placed in the 5th house of "Nobody Does It Better," this karmic debt appears to be the result of a previous lifetime in which your celebrity status and pleasurable lifestyle were achieved through the self-serving abuse and/or lazy neglect of powerful authority, romantic love, or creative talent. In this somewhat egotistical existence, you dominated those who looked to you for leadership by arrogantly reaping the creative fruits of their individual labors. No wonder yesterday's guilt can be so easily invoked by today's personal creations, especially your offspring. Although frequently compelled by your weakness for romance and your aptitude for the performing arts, your karmic payback in the here and now requires your unselfish service in giving others the creative recognition they deserve and the joyful sense of fun they so desperately need. If not, expect a painful loss in the areas of life that determine your own.

In particular, any of your experiences with children, love affairs, romance, personal creativity, play, drama, art, leisure activities, recreation/sports, investments/gambling.

Neptune in the 6th House

Universal Payback: Your Everyday Life

With natal Neptune placed in the 6th house of the "Daily Grind," this karmic debt appears to be the result of a previous lifetime in which the menial tasks of everyday work and the routine responsibilities of physical health were abused, unappreciated, or neglected. With unrealistic standards of excellence that could never be achieved, you made those who served your everyday needs suffer severely with both the mental humiliation and the physical debilitation of inadequacy. Is it any wonder you have so many mysterious ailments today when you inflicted so much inferiority yesterday? Although frequently compelled by unconscious habits and ill-advised diets, your karmic payback in the here and now requires your unselfish service in performing the necessary tasks and practical duties that are so desperately needed by others. If not, expect a painful loss in the areas of life that contribute to your own.

In particular, any of your experiences with coworkers, pets, service providers, daily work, health, nutrition, physical fitness, routine tasks, daily exercises, maintenance procedures.

Neptune in the 7th House

Universal Payback: Your Others

With natal Neptune placed in the 7th house of "Couples Only," this karmic debt appears to be the result of a previous lifetime in which the mutual commitment of meaningful mergers, business alliances, and marital unions was emotionally abused and/or carelessly neglected. In some manipulative way, you used your idealistic expectations of love and equality to control your significant relationships, dominate your legal partnerships, or exploit your contractual agreements by evoking a deep sense of inadequacy in others. Not surprisingly, yesterday's lack of emotional commitment attracts today's unrewarding relationships. Although you're often compelled by an unconscious sense of unrealistic obligation in your partnerships, your karmic payback in the here and now requires your unselfish service in providing others with the equity and balance that their significant relationships so desperately need. If not, expect a painful loss in the areas of life that enhance your own.

In particular, any of your experiences with partners, clients, adversaries, opponents, society, the public, lawyers, contracts, negotiations, legal affairs.

Neptune in the 8th House

Universal Payback: Your Shared Stuff

With natal Neptune placed in the 8th house of "What's Yours Is Mine Too," this karmic debt appears to be the result of a previous lifetime in which the powerful control of joint resources, untapped reserves, and life-and-death issues was dangerously abused and/or carelessly neglected. Accountable for the property and secrets of others, your covert, manipulative, or paranoid desire for dominance led to the financial ruin, emotional devastation, or physical destruction of all concerned. No wonder today's partners and liaisons never give you the intimacy you desire or the funding you need. Although frequently compelled by your intuitive sense of emotional or psychological manipulation, your karmic payback in the here and now demands your unselfish service in helping others access the hidden resources they so desperately need for survival. If not, expect a painful loss in the areas of life that define your own.

In particular, any of your experiences with sex, intimacy, death, conception, partner's resources, other people's money, joint assets, inheritances, insurance, taxes.

Neptune in the 9th House

Universal Payback: Your New Horizons

With natal Neptune placed in the 9th house of the "Big Picture," this karmic debt appears to be the result of a previous lifetime in which your responsibility for pursuing knowledge, spreading truth, or promoting justice was self-righteously abused and/or carelessly neglected. By imposing your own philosophical beliefs, political opinions, or spiritual convictions on others, you inhibited the growth and limited the learning of those you were supposed to inspire. No wonder today's higher education always seems to get obstructed by yesterday's intellectual superiority. Although compelled by an unconscious wanderlust to move beyond the boundaries of your childhood limitations, your karmic payback in the here and now requires your unselfish service in helping others expand both their minds and their horizons to obtain the enlightenment they long for. If not, expect a painful loss in the areas of life that define your own.

In particular, any of your experiences with in-laws, foreigners, court decisions, college, higher education, religion/philosophies, broadcasting, publishing, long distance travels.

Neptune in the 10th House

Universal Payback: Your Public World

With natal Neptune placed in the 10th house of "Worldly Ambition," this karmic debt appears to be the result of a previous lifetime in which the official responsibilities of parental authority, professional career, or public reputation were severely abused and/or carelessly neglected. Those under your authority suffered severely when your ruthless ambition for success and status led to either the humiliating loss of your professional reputation or the shameful disgrace of a very public scandal. No wonder today's authority figures are never emotionally available. Although frequently compelled by a strong sense of your own destiny, your karmic payback in the here and now requires your unselfish service in helping others work within the established rules of organized structure to earn the respect they deserve. If not, expect a painful loss in the areas of life that contribute to your own.

In particular, any of your experiences with father, authority figures, superiors, public image, public reputation, professional status, professional career, professional ambition, politics.

Neptune in the 11th House

Universal Payback: Your Social Life

With natal Neptune placed in the 11th house of "Plays Well With Others," this karmic debt appears to be the result of a previous lifetime in which the humanitarian ideals of social reform and universal brotherhood were radically abused and/or stubbornly neglected. Friends and associates suffered severely from the social unrest or community chaos that was provoked by either your revolutionary behavior or your antisocial attitudes. No wonder your guilt over yesterday's victims attracts all those disappointing colleagues today. Although frequently compelled by your highly developed intuition and advanced technological visions, your karmic payback in the here and now requires your unselfish service in working effectively as a group member to change the status quo for those who are in desperate need of improved social conditions. If not, expect a painful loss in the areas of life that define your own.

In particular, any of your experiences with friends, peers, colleagues, social circles, humanitarian ideals, vision, future goals, hopes and wishes, clubs/associations, group accomplishments, rebellions.

Neptune in the 12th House

Universal Payback: Your Eternal Life

With natal Neptune placed here in the private sanctuary of the soul, this karmic debt appears to be the result of a previous lifetime in which the subliminal escapes of unconditional faith, creative imagination, and the unconscious past were severely abused and/or carelessly neglected. It seems those who relied on your emotional support suffered severely when you fell victim to your own self-inflicted isolation, guilt, or martyrdom after being overwhelmed by the harsh realities of life. No wonder yesterday's self-imposed confinement evokes today's deep-seated loneliness. Although you're often undermined by an extreme vulnerability to drugs, allergies, and alcohol, your karmic payback in the here and now requires providing the real victims of the world with the compassionate support they truly deserve and the psychological rehabilitation they so desperately need. If not, expect a painful loss in the areas of life that contribute to your own.

In particular, any of your experiences with soul, faith, spirituality, religion, mental health, addictions, dependencies, illegal activities, institutions, prisons/hospitals, secrets, the unconscious past, karma/past lives.

7

Pluto: Your Karmic Arsenal

The true beginning of our end.

—WILLIAM SHAKESPEARE

Most people know that Pluto, the ninth and last known planet in our solar system, wasn't discovered until February 18, 1930, but what few people realize is that this scientific event occurred only months after the stock market crashed, setting off a worldwide economic depression, and only weeks into the decade that would soon be giving us the rise of Adolph Hitler, Al Capone, and World War II. When a universal energy named for the Roman god of the underworld finally orbits its way out of the astronomical unknown and into our conscious awareness, it's bound to make a formidable impact on the world and, because of that, a powerful difference in our lives.

That is exactly what Pluto did and precisely why it was named the astrological planet of change and transformation. With a distance from the earth that proved to be almost fifty times greater than the earth's distance from the Sun, this planet was almost impossible to find in 1930, let alone study. In fact, the first astrologers to observe Pluto were forced to base its influence in the natal chart entirely on what they could see of its behavior through the lens of a telescope, which in those days and at that distance was little more than nothing. Keeping astronomers in the dark is apparently what put Pluto in control, and that's where it's been ever since, making the ninth planet in our solar system the most formidable planet in the horoscope. This dark and mysterious planet was up there stealing its tiny way around the Sun from what could only be the deepest corners of the cosmos, while soaking up what could only be the darkest secrets of the universe for centuries before anyone down here in the math and science department even knew it existed. No wonder modern astrologers determined Pluto to be the guardian of the soul and the ruler of our subconscious. Without the knowledge of anyone, Pluto was actually out there bringing the power of the great unknown to everyone by secretly exposing us to all the dark and light, good and evil, higher and lower forces of heaven and hell that went with it—the universal forces of creation and destruction. Astrologers had to be impressed. They also had to be a little awed because, as far as they were concerned, these were the spiritual forces of transformation, and apparently, as far as the guardian of our soul was concerned, we were going to need them.

Before we go any further, and before giving anyone a chance to confuse Pluto, the guardian of our soul, with Neptune, the ruler of our soul, let's take a minute to clarify the difference between these two karmic influences and their spiritual job descriptions. Neptune is the planet that *rules our unconscious self* and, because of that, reflects the memory of yesterday's guilt and ecstasy. Pluto is the planet that *guards our subconscious self* and, because it does, reflects the impact of today's powerful desires. Weak or strong, Neptune is the energy that inspires us. Good or bad, Pluto is the influence that empowers us. Astrologically speaking, Neptune is our soul and Pluto is our conscience.

That makes sense when you think about what Pluto brings to the astrological party. Power—and not just any kind of power—the kind that only initiates new beginnings because it always creates death-like endings, the kind of power that should have a conscience behind it. This is why Pluto's placement in the natal chart can't help but reveal where we have the powerful ability to transform others. Its presence in the natal sky reflects where we promised the cosmos we'd transform ourselves first. Yes, you should have seen that one coming, but if you didn't, then here it is. Natal Pluto is our earthly commitment to become a more powerful person in this lifetime because it reflects our soul's karmic promise to protect others from whatever it was that left us feeling so powerless in the last one. While this may be a noble concept, it's a risky practice because, as great as it sounds, it's impossible to achieve without first getting access to all those forces out there that are greater than our own, all the people, things, and influences that are more powerful than we are. Because more powerful forces are even harder to manipulate than they are to come by, the cosmos knew we were going to need more than just a little astrological help finding these resources—we were going to need a lot of universal help controlling them. Powerful choices always have powerful consequences, which, by the way, is not only what brought a conscience into our soul's spiritual picture eons ago but, because of that, what brings Pluto into our astrological one today—and into your natal chart.

Sign first, of course. That's because, just like every other planet in the solar system, the constellation Pluto occupied at your birth is a celestial documentation of a job well done in a previous life, universal recognition of a time when your soul rose to the cosmic occasion and served its earthly purpose above and beyond the call of spiritual duty—your karmic kudos. Because Pluto takes 249 years to complete one orbit around the Sun and spends more than twenty years in each constellation, entire generations are born during each of Pluto's journeys through a particular sign. There's a reason for that. Many astrologers call it a "generational influence" and, astrologically speaking, that's what it is. From a karmic perspective, however, it's because at one challenging time in the difficult past, this generation of souls shared the same life-changing crisis, catastrophe, or power struggle—quite possibly one in which they lost their mortal lives. Because each of them rose to the occasion back then, they all share the same universal talent for accessing Pluto's power today, which is why, as a group, they now share the same Pluto sign—mass karma, if you will. For instance, in:

Cancer: Through family upheavals, domestic power struggles, and patriotic causes.

Leo: Through wars, leadership upheavals, or power struggles over artistic creativity, romantic love, or talented children.

Virgo: Through medical upheavals, physical health crisis, and government catastrophes.

Libra: Through social upheavals in arbitration, law, diplomacy, and marriage.

Scorpio: Through natural disasters and catastrophic emergencies due to wars, plagues, diseases, and evil forces.

Sagittarius: Through intellectual upheavals in scientific and political thought, spiritual values, and fundamental philosophy.

Capricorn: Through professional power struggles, political upheavals, and public scandal.

Aquarius: Through upheavals in humanitarianism, scientific discovery, and universal brotherhood.

While it's insightful to know just how we earned the power to transform ourselves in the past, the real Pluto story lies in where the cosmos is waiting for us to do it now. That brings us into our own natal chart and right up to the front door of our Pluto house—what I like to call our very own astrological arsenal, because this is where we keep all the psychological strengths and passionate desires that we are now authorized to use as our powerful inner resources when it's time for transformation. Not coincidently, these just happen to be the same strengths and desires we instinctively choose to unleash as our emotional weapons of retaliation when we're faced with something more important, like a deep need for vengeance. This is why Pluto's house placement in the natal chart identifies the very people, places, and things that we now have the ability to emotionally influence or psychologically control in this life. These are the untapped resources that the universe has made available to us so that we can get the job done—for good or, if we're nursing a grudge, for evil. It is our conscience, our job choice.

Either way, our Pluto house reveals just where in life we will always be able to get to the heart of any matter and the root of every issue because this house identifies just what it is that incites us to research, investigate, and detect with a passion that is unmatched by anyone. On our darker Pluto days, it triggers us to manipulate, detonate, and annihilate with the fury of a nuclear explosion, which is really not all that uncommon in a place where purpose and passion have access to all the right power (Pluto's) for all the wrong reasons (ours). In fact, it's through the events and circumstances of this very house that, one way or another, Pluto will force us to regenerate our lives, resurrect our past, and, in some meaningful way, rebuild ourselves. We have to. This is where we agreed to focus the powers of our profound purpose and intense passion on something other than our own obsessions, like a few deep and miraculous transformations, starting with the up-close-and-personal kind: our own.

That's a good thing, even if it doesn't always feel that way—not just because a long time ago our soul made a promise to suck it up and overcome whatever controlled us in a previous life, but because wielding our own power wisely is the only way to accomplish a task like that in this life. Besides, with all that Plutonian energy we have at our human disposal down here, it's good to know that Pluto is up there keeping us from killing each other with it. In a perfect world maybe, but this is planet earth, and it's far from perfect. In fact, that's why the cosmos sent us down here to begin with and why Pluto was put in charge of controlling all the powerful forces of nature on it. We were given a conscience, but we were also given the choices and, sadly, lots of misguided passion. This is why we'd be wise to remember that although Pluto's promise of power is always assured in the birth chart, its methods are never less than extreme in the real world—our world. While Pluto demands that we get the life-changing makeover we promised to get, it also insists that the only real path to our transformation, and everybody else's, is complete and absolute destruction. That's why we're getting all the power to begin with. According to the Pluto principle, we can't really create anything new without first eliminating the old. In fact, it's that very principle that makes natal Pluto more than just our astrological authorization to life-changing power. It's our promise to the universe that, one way or another, we will create a powerful new us, which means that in every birth chart natal Pluto is really just our own personal karmic slate waiting to be wiped clean. Fortunately for the rest of the world, each one comes with a conscience.

Pluto in the 1st House

Although you're instinctively drawn to powerful people and magnetic personalities, you're often just as instinctively compelled to dominate them. This is because you've chosen to become physically powerful in this lifetime to keep from being brutally dominated by stronger individuals as you were in the past. With this 1st house Pluto, however, you must demonstrate your strength and independence with actions that are physically courageous, not violently destructive. This means you must now protect yourself and others with ambitions that are personally responsible, not passionately self-indulgent. Your new beginnings will only occur when you're able to conquer your inner demons, and thus eliminate our biggest bully. Despite what you think, in this Pluto house survival is not your path to power. Leadership is.

Transformation Triggers: Your physical body, your inner child, your superego, and anyone else who shows up in your mirror—or worse, gets in your way.

Pluto in the 2nd House

No wonder your desires for wealth, property, and financial gain can be so intense that at times almost everything else seems meaningless. You've chosen to become empowered in this lifetime by the one thing that controlled you completely in the past: money. Before that's possible, however, this 2nd house Pluto insists that you resurrect your values, regenerate your resources, and rethink your priorities. Evidently, your powerful new beginnings depend on more than just being able to get your hands on everything that happens to be worth anything. You must be willing to give up one valuable asset to attain another. In fact, only then will you finally be able to prove to the world what you came into it believing. Wealth is power.

Transformation Triggers: Money, every material possession you own, money, every material possession someone else owns, money, every material possession you want to own. And, oh yes, money.

Pluto in the 3rd House

It's not surprising that you have such keen powers of observation and such a penetrating mind. You were controlled by information in a previous incarnation and now regard it as essential in terms of the power it gives you over others and, more importantly, them over you. That is why this 3rd house Pluto insists that you exercise great caution when handling the intimate communications or the classified data of others. Apparently, you must now use the power of words and ideas to demonstrate to the community that the pen really is mightier than the sword. New beginnings depend on your ability to keep both the secrets you're empowered by and the ones you're entrusted with. In this Pluto house, knowledge is power.

Transformation Triggers: The siblings, neighbors, and classmates who are stupid enough to think they're smarter than you, and anyone else in the world who actually is.

Pluto in the 4th House

In one way or another you will always find yourself returning home to your family roots in this lifetime as you have chosen to overcome the very same childhood trauma or domestic powerlessness that controlled you in a previous one. In order to do so, however, this 4th house Pluto insists that you protect yourself and create a more powerful sense of belongingness for others by exposing family secrets, unearthing old resentments, and eliminating domestic abuses—not burying them. Or, worse, creating new ones. In some meaningful way, you must now renew the family or transform the domestic scene, not dominate it. Your transformations occur through the bloodline, real estate, or roots of your family. In this house, your history has power.

Transformation Triggers: The woman who raised you, the country you came from, and any man, woman, or child that you've ever been related to.

Pluto in the 5th House

No wonder this 5th house Pluto gives you no other choice but to seek outlets that allow you to express yourself creatively. You've chosen to be empowered in this lifetime by the brilliant talents and burning passions that enslaved you to others in the past. This means you must now reawaken the artistic genius in others by creatively regenerating your own. That can only be achieved by using your own powerful urges to passionately inspire ours, not emotionally manipulate us, or worse, destroy yourself. Evidently your new beginnings occur by taking a creative risk with talent, not a dangerous one with life, yours or anyone else's. In this Pluto house, the power is all creative, which means, in the real world, your creations are all-powerful.

Transformation Triggers: Talented children, powerful lovers, and all those financial investments that prove to be neither.

Pluto in the 6th House

You are intensely serious about your work and health because you have decided to become more powerful in this lifetime by repairing the very same inefficiencies or physical ailments that left you feeling incapable, unproductive, and powerless in the past. To do so, however, this 6th house Pluto insists that you now develop the specialized skills or acquire the technical knowledge that will in some way improve the quality of our daily lives today. That means you must now protect yourself and empower others by providing both the practical service we desperately need and the physical perfection you inherently crave. Your new beginnings occur by reinventing the reality of physical fitness, not obsessing over it. In this house, physical service is power.

Transformation Triggers: Every tyrannical boss, overbearing coworker, abusive employee, or unforeseen health risk that you have to face in the workplace, or worse, we have to face in you.

Pluto in the 7th House

You can't help but attract partners that are strong-willed, domineering, and manipulative. You've chosen to become a more powerful significant other in this lifetime by overcoming the same emotionally abusive relationships that controlled you in a previous one. That is why this 7th house Pluto insists that you now protect yourself and defend others by doing whatever it takes to destroy oppression, build trust, and create balance in relationships—anything legal and moral, that is. Your new beginnings depend on objectively eliminating contention and lawfully reinstating equality for those who need it, not manipulating or forfeiting your own. In fact, you must never give away anything to a partner that you're unable to demand for yourself. In this house, equality is power.

Transformation Triggers: Unbearable spouses, unmovable partners, unbreakable contracts, and every unscrupulous lawyer behind them.

Pluto in the 8th House

Despite being instilled with an indomitable life force and such a strong sense of purpose, at times you can be so overwhelmed by cynicism and despair that you become annoyingly defensive and preoccupied with survival. You've chosen to master the same critical influences and catastrophic forces of nature in this incarnation that left you abandoned, exposed, or powerless in the past. No wonder this 8th house Pluto insists that you now regenerate yourself and protect others through the shrewd management of life-changing resources. Death and vulnerability are not an option. Evidently, your new beginnings must be created by uncovering powerful reserves, accessing unconditional trust, and skillfully controlling both—not abusing or manipulating either. In this Pluto house, intimacy is power.

Transformation Triggers: Your first encounters with death, your early encounters with sex, and your every encounter with the IRS.

Pluto in the 9th House

This 9th house Pluto instills such a strong desire for truth, justice, and adventure that you're not only compelled to understand foreign cultures, explore distant places, and discover new philosophies, you're profoundly affected by them whenever you do, primarily because you've decided that becoming intellectually empowered in this lifetime would effectively eliminate all the spiritual, academic, and physical boundaries that were imposed on you in the past. While that can't be achieved without fearlessly investigating the unknown and bravely realizing the impossible, your new beginnings won't really occur until you're able to enlighten everyone with your findings without intimidating anyone with your beliefs. Apparently, your moral views must inspire others, not dominate them. In this Pluto house, intellectual freedom is power.

Transformation Tiggers: Overbearing opinions, and all the overbearing teachers, ministers, foreigners, or in-laws who insist on shoving them down your throat.

Pluto in the 10th House

Although you're intensely reluctant to relinquish control over your life to any authority figure in it, you're just as intensely attracted to people in public office and positions of social power. You've chosen to become a powerful, prominent figure yourself in this incarnation in order to overcome the manipulation or abuse you suffered at the hands of superiors in the past. Unfortunately, before you can advance in the outside world, this 10th house Pluto insists that you now protect yourself and others from the destructive evils in it. This means your new beginnings depend on your ability to openly work within the rules of professional society to somehow transform it, not dominate us. In this house, public status is power.

Transformation Triggers: The rules that must be followed, the regulations that can't be broken, and all the parents, bosses, politicians, and control freaks that keep bringing them to your attention.

Pluto in the 11th House

You will always regard your friendships with important people and your memberships in prominent organizations as valuable resources for gaining personal power. They are. You have chosen to become a more powerful member of society in this lifetime by affiliating yourself with only those individuals who can help you reform the very same social conditions that destroyed or controlled you in the past. That is why this 11th house Pluto insists that you now protect yourself and revolutionize society by reinventing it, and that means skillfully rubbing elbows with the people and pastimes that empower your idealistic goals, not manipulating and abusing them, or worse, destroying you. Your new beginnings require your best associations. In this house, social participation is power.

Transformation Triggers: The powerful friends you don't know, and the treacherous ones you think you do.

Pluto in the 12th House

You can't help but seek to expand your personal awareness and develop your subconscious abilities. You've chosen to become a more powerful soul in this lifetime because you've agreed to regenerate and heal those painful emotional experiences and traumatic psychological events that kept you and your soul confined for lifetimes. That is why this 12th house Pluto insists that you now protect yourself and rehabilitate others by uncovering the unconscious secrets, examining the emotional afflictions, and understanding the psychological weaknesses that traumatized you in the past. And

8

The 12th House: Your Karmic Closet

O! that I were as great as is my grief,
Or lesser than my name,
Or that I could forget what I have been,
Or not remember what I must be now.

—WILLIAM SHAKESPEARE

Welcome to the 12th house of your natal chart or, as I like to refer to it, the Petri dish for your karmic DNA. For those of you who are not familiar with this section of the horoscope, the 12th house represents the final stage of life and, for obvious reasons, is said to be the astrological home of the soul. To most astrologers, it's that place on the birth map that mirrors your spiritual development and karmic journey, simply because to every astrologer it reflects that point in the universe that harbors your unconscious past. This is the part of your natal chart where the inner you keeps the memory and imprint of all that you were before, all that you are below the surface, and all that is not apparent. Evidently, like still waters, the 12th house runs very deep. It's supposed to.

While some of our gloomier stargazers refer to this last piece of the birth puzzle as the house of secrets, sorrows, and self-undoing, there are others who see it as the house of dreams, faith, and destiny. It has lots of labels, but the fact of the astrological matter is, the 12th house lives up to all of them for one reason only. It's a portal to the past—your past. Intrigued? Well, you should be. When it comes to this neck of the natal neighborhood, you should also be a little cautious, not just because the cosmos assigned that mystical constellation Pisces and its ambiguous ruling planet Neptune to be our official 12th house astrological landlords, but because, according to karmic code, nothing under their roof is ever what it appears to be. Nothing clear, definite, or realistic is allowed behind these woeful walls to begin with, which is precisely why your perspective will always be severely compromised anytime you start poking around back there yourself. Sorry, house rules, so if you're looking for answers, enter at your own risk, but not without exercising a little cosmic caution. If there's one thing every astrologer agrees on, it's that the 12th house is the only place in the natal chart that can be as misleading as it is enlightening. The same can be said for the past.

Whenever we explore this last house of our natal chart, we unknowingly open the locked closet of the soul and venture directly into Neptune and Pisces territory. It's here in this bygone haunt of painful memories and precious experiences that our soul stores the blueprint for each one of our previous, and in some way, painful, triumphs, misdeeds, and unconscious habit patterns. As a result, the 12th house is always somewhat foreboding, deceptive, secretive, and intoxicating, which, of course, accounts for our fascination. Neptune and Pisces wouldn't have it any other way. While they may not insist we wipe our feet before crossing their threshold, you can bet that when we hit their turf, we'll be expected to escape, sacrifice, and bleed with the best of them, and we will—we really have no choice. That's because whenever we direct our attention to this house, we're compelled to address both the dreams and the nightmares of our most recent past, those very images that made us what we are today by constantly reminding us of what we never got around to being yesterday. Ah, memories. Then why do we even bother with this house anyway? Because we have to, because this is where our soul buried all the behaviors, attitudes, strengths, and weaknesses that once upon another lifetime were just too unbearable for us to deal with—or perhaps impossible to live up to. These are the same painful issues and idiosyncrasies that we must face in this lifetime because they are the same painful pieces of the past that, for one reason or another, we refused to deal with in the last one—all the things we never saw for what they really were, only what we wanted them to be or, in many cases, what we turned them into. In fact, we went further than just not facing the things we stuck in this karmic closet, we actually buried them, but only after we spent a good part of our last lifetime denying, ignoring, or drowning in them. That is why we made a promise to confront them now—not to heal, fix, or embrace them, not even to conquer them, but simply to open that closet, bring them out into the open, and, once and for all, stop hiding them. The only way to keep these improperly programmed memories from inhibiting us spiritually and crippling us psychologically is to move them out of the dark and unconscious corners of our 12th house and into a more conscious part of our lives, the part of our lives where they no longer have the power to undermine us—the daylight part of our lives, the any-other-house-but-the-12th part.

Now as much as that sounds like a whole lot of fun, it should be remembered that the soul will always have a difficult time resisting the temptation to connect or merge with anything familiar, whether it be a person, a situation, or a wound. Because everything in the 12th house was put there by the soul, every time we allow ourselves to open that intriguing door, or even peer through its karmic peephole, our indiscriminate soul can't help but surrender to all those wistful yearnings of its familiar past. That's exactly when we can't help but conveniently avoid all the things we should be doing in the unfamiliar present—important things like shining bright in our Sun house, learning our Saturn lesson, or even just dodging Neptune's nudges—things we end up not doing. After all, when you carelessly rekindle the heartaches of yesterday, they're bound to become the unavoidable priorities of today and, because of that, our inevitable misery tomorrow. No wonder you can't go home again.

Is there anything more self-destructive than embracing the inadequacies that plagued us in the past, while at the same time neglecting the very talents we spent a previous lifetime wasting? Of course not, but this is the 12th house, remember? What could be more Pisces-like than following in our own karmic footprints or, for that matter, more Neptune-like than not even knowing that we're doing it? Nothing. Hence, the past becomes the future and history repeats itself. Our history—enter secrets, sorrows, and self-undoing.

Is it really any wonder why the 12th house gets such bad press? It shouldn't be—not when it's the only place in our natal charts where we intuitively preserve yesterday yet seem to helplessly neglect tomorrow, where vice is frequently mistaken for virtue, and sinking always feels like swimming—our own personal haunted house with optional doorways to either possible sainthood or inevitable sin. Why? Because in true Neptunian fashion, it's the only place where our spiritual future depends on our human ability to confront the memories of yesterday without mind, body, or spirit getting nostalgically sucked back into them today. You're supposed to be confused. It's the house rules, remember? Besides, how could we ever understand any place where we can be deceived and victimized just as frequently as we are gifted and inspired? It's impossible, but also quite typical because Pisces and Neptune would never tolerate anyone understanding their little piece of the universe. They only insist we address it and only when we become serious about finding the one thing that never comes looking for us: enlightenment. That's why the constellation placed on this house at the moment of our birth is their ambiguous way of reminding us of our strengths and warning us of our weaknesses, while burying both in our unconscious. Again, house rules. Fortunately, we only have to look at our birth charts from that higher perspective to see that this sign's ruling planet is also somewhere in the horoscope providing some powerful insight into where we should be going by shedding a little cosmic light on exactly where we came from. This, by the way, just happens to be both the fundamental purpose and the primary lesson of the 12th house. If we expect to embrace our future, we must first relinquish our past. Ironically, in this illusionary and confusing house, the real difficulty lies in being able to tell the difference between the two—compliments of Pisces and Neptune, of course.

Aries in the 12th House: Mars Rules

Your soul's previous existence was one of personal independence and physical ambition. Although you were a real force to be reckoned with in this past incarnation, a debilitating personal defeat forced you to bury your self-esteem here in the house of "now you see it, now you don't." As a result, your powerful ego always escapes initial detection in this life, which is why you are surprisingly aggressive, much more competitive than you appear, and secretly burdened by unconscious anger from the past. Unfortunately, if this buried fury is left unaddressed, it becomes a lethal disadvantage to you as well as a concealed danger to others. While your capable past has left you with both an ability to operate skillfully behind the scenes and a preference for secret planning or covert activities, it has also instilled in you an aptness for deeper mind subjects such as hypnosis, dreams, or psychology. Your profound courage and instinctive decisiveness are truly your hidden strengths, but the impatient ego that comes with them is likely to cause as much undoing in this lifetime as it did previously. Passion is your weakness. Predictably, however, sex and physical activity are your addictions. A decided effort must be made to stop unconsciously avoiding the leadership roles you desire by being drawn to dangerous situations or confrontational people. Past influences and experiences include physical competition, law enforcement, martial arts, weaponry, the military, politics, psychology, or surgery. You can be a deadly bully in sheep's clothing.

Cosmic Advice: Stay away from sharp objects in the hands of angry adversaries.

Taurus in the 12th House: Venus Rules

Your soul's previous existence was one of personal pleasure, material abundance, and tangible productivity. This affluent lifestyle came with a price, however, as your personal values had to be suppressed in this past incarnation for the sake of physical comfort or material security. As a result, your talents, affections, and happiness are now very profound and deeply inhibited. This is not only why you are actually more kind, sympathetic, and vulnerable than you appear, but also why you are highly susceptible to flattery and a real pushover for anyone who offers security. With an almost obsessive affinity for taste, touch, and texture, you're also a lot more sensual than you would like others to know. Not surprisingly, physical pleasure is your weakness because sensual satisfaction is your addiction. Obviously, old habits die hard and denial is not easily relinquished as your past inability to see the flaws in others has left you prone to deception and disappointment in love affairs today. Your strong value system is truly your hidden strength, although, one way or another, beautiful objects, valuable possessions, and cold hard cash will continue to be as much of an undoing in this life as they were in the past. Your repressed artistic abilities must be nourished if you are to stop unconsciously avoiding the material wealth and financial stability you claim to be seeking. Past influences and experiences include art, music, design, banking, farming, construction, and architecture. You're more determined than we know and more stubborn than you think.

Cosmic Advice: Lose the guilt. It makes you lazy and drives us crazy.

Gemini in the 12th House: Mercury Rules

Your soul's previous existence was one of mental stimulation and community networking. Highly intellectual in this past incarnation, your overwhelming guilt forced you to bury your intellect when the ideas, information, or communications you exchanged led to severe loss or confinement. While this mental suppression left you unsure of your ability to articulate clearly or express your thoughts effectively, you now have an acute link to the unconscious mind. In fact, you not only reason better when you're exhausted, you also have a keen sense of intuition, very vivid dreams, and a gift for extrasensory perception. Your thinking actually operates on the unconscious level, making your insightful impressions more instinctual than logical. Apparently, the past has left you with a profound desire to inform that explains both your inability to keep a secret and that annoying little habit you have of exposing whatever it is that should remain concealed. Not surprisingly, irresponsible communications were the cause of your past undoing. Even less surprisingly, they're still somewhat of a problem this time around. Your adaptability and intellect are truly your hidden strengths. Intense curiosity and a compulsion for gossip are unquestionably your destructive weaknesses. You probably suffered the loss of a twin or sibling in the past and now unconsciously avoid close sibling relationships by assuming the role of fraternal doormat. Past influences and experiences include teaching, writing, journalism, commerce, academics, communications, and transportation.

Cosmic Advice: Stop being so nosy. There are some things that even you don't need to know.

Cancer in the 12th House: Moon Rules

Your soul's previous existence called for the guardianship of home, family, country, or the ancestral past. Unfortunately, however, your care and watchful attention had to be suppressed in this past incarnation for the sake of emotional nourishment or domestic security. As a result, your parental instincts and feelings of devotion are now very profound, which is why your remarkable survival skills, unwavering patriotism, and superior nurturing abilities are rarely obvious until tested. It is also why, despite your ability to seem unaffected by criticism and rejection, you are surprisingly moody and more vulnerable than you appear. Without question, loyalty and tenacity are your hidden strengths. Without question, food and drink are your weaknesses. Your inability to "let go" of old pain was the cause of your previous undoing and, unfortunately, the odds-on favorite for your misery in this life as well. The past has left you with a deep need for intimacy that now manifests as an attachment to privacy, secrecy, or seclusion in both your domestic life and your relationships, which explains why you unconsciously avoid the happy home and loving family you desire by suffocating those around you with what you call concern and the rest of us call smothering. Deeply affected by your mother and childhood, you clearly have a karmic connection to one or both parents, but you knew that. Past influences and experiences include patriot, historian, genealogist, chef, homemaker, shopkeeper, or landlord.

Cosmic Advice: Give up the grudges. Some memories are not worth keeping.

Leo in the 12th House: Sun Rules

Your soul's previous existence was one of personal distinction, creative brilliance, and courageous leadership. Unfortunately, this past incarnation left your self-esteem so bruised, your ego had no alternative but to bury itself here in the house of "let's deal with it later." This explains why your ability to dominate so completely and to govern so effectively is now so well concealed. In fact, your astonishing influence and tremendous willpower are both your hidden strengths and your secret weapons as they are never obvious until we have to deal with them. While a powerful ego and excessive pride were the cause of your past undoing, it seems they can be just as overbearing and troublesome this time around. Your passion for love and romance is your addiction. When it lures you into those secret trysts and forbidden affairs, it's your dangerous weakness.

You work best alone, independently or in a secluded setting, as the past has left you with an aversion to being responsible for others. Thus, you now unconsciously avoid positions of leadership, authority, and parenthood by either relying on partners for income, suppressing your creativity, or attracting unhealthy romances. Deeply affected by your father and any other figures of authority, your own power in this lifetime tends to involve healing, confinement, or the unconscious past. Surprisingly, you are often the power behind the throne. Not surprisingly, it's your best-kept secret. Past influences and experiences include ruler, politician, royalty, leader, entertainer, artist, or teacher.

Cosmic Advice: If you really want the applause, you'll have to get into the spotlight.

Virgo in the 12th House: Mercury Rules

Your soul's previous existence was one of physical duty and practical service to others. Dedicated to the highest degree of excellence in this past incarnation, your inability to achieve some type of physical perfection forced you to bury your keen intellect here in the house of "whose inadequacy is it, anyway." Hence, you are now constantly compelled to defend your sharp analytical abilities and your logical solutions, as they never seem to get the credit they deserve. Clearly this is your baggage, but when your critical thinking has been so severely suppressed, the mental baggage is bound to be abundant. Surprisingly observant, your organization and research skills are profound and instinctive. Deep devotion to the painstaking details that are so frequently neglected by others is your hidden strength.

Work, health, and fitness are your addictions, but only because being useful is your weakness. While excessive worry and chronic faultfinding were the cause of your past undoing, they appear to be back for a repeat performance. The past has left you with an overwhelming sense of duty to repair the inevitable flaws of reality. Unfortunately, this unconscious fixation with perfection can actually cause you to avoid the ideal efficiency you seek by drawing you to flawed data, disorganized people, and impossible situations. You can stop wondering why we're so incompetent and you're so neurotic. Past influences and experiences include teaching, writing, critical analysis, accounting, medicine, engineering, and craftsmanship.

Cosmic Advice: Stop worrying. You're still alive and the sky isn't falling.

Libra in the 12th House: Venus Rules

Your soul's previous existence was one of cooperation and partnership. Somewhat weak and dependent in this past incarnation, you buried your happiness here in the bargain basement of the birth chart by using marriage or partnership as a means of escape. Your self-esteem was sacrificed, your love confined, and your talents suppressed as you were victimized in some abusive or even masochistic way for what you thought would be a life of luxury and security. This not only explains why you are now so highly susceptible to flattery and affection, but also why these controlling relationships are not necessarily a thing of the past. Obviously, your passion for partnership is your addiction. Sadly, your dependency on others is your weakness.

You harbor artistic abilities or musical talents that were severely repressed in the past and discouraged again in this life by either rejection, loss, or criticism. Manipulating others with your wealth or beauty was the cause of your previous undoing. Remarkable diplomatic skills and a strong sense of justice are your hidden strengths. The past instilled a deep need to enhance your status and strengthen your persona by attaching yourself to a powerful player. Not surprisingly, you unconsciously avoid that ideal marriage or relationship by being drawn to dominant partners and manipulative people. So much martyrdom, so little time. Past influences and experiences include music, fine arts, design, modeling, public relations, diplomacy, or law. You're more vain than you think and more strategic than we know.

Cosmic Advice: If you really want power, stop sacrificing it for peace.

Scorpio in the 12th House: Pluto Rules

Your soul's previous existence was one of surviving the powerful and unknown forces of nature. In this past incarnation, the life-changing consequences of sex, death, or catastrophe left you dependent on the charity of others and harboring a profound feeling of powerlessness. Survival had to be the priority so vulnerability had to go. Thus, your overwhelming experiences of either emotional abuse, physical violence, or drastic separation were deeply buried and dangerously neglected. Not surprisingly, exceptional courage and fierce determination are now your hidden strengths. As a result, you developed incredible instincts and phenomenal crisis management skills that enable you to uncover powerful reserves and cleverly handle the property or secrets of others. You know how to get to the bottom of anything, which keeps you on top of everything. While shared assets and secret liaisons were responsible for your previous undoing, they seem to be the escape routes of choice in this lifetime as well.

Yes, passion is your weakness, but your real addiction is control. While the past has left you with both a deep need for powerful intimacy and an instinctive, yet hair-trigger defense system, you often avoid one and undermine the other by taking drastic measures to protect yourself from ever being controlled by anyone, but only because death would be more acceptable. Previous influences and experiences include detective work, forensics, chemistry, military, surgery, psychology, or archaeology. You never fear anyone but always suspect everyone.

Cosmic Advice: Buried resentments are backyard karmic land mines. Dig them up or they'll destroy you.

Sagittarius in the 12th House: Jupiter Rules

Your soul's previous existence was one of abundant good fortune and deep philosophic beliefs. Dedicated to the pursuit and promotion of truth and enlightenment in this past incarnation, your spirited crusades for justice, adventurous quests for knowledge, and staunch campaigns for the underdog inspired others to move beyond the limits of their existing boundaries. Unfortunately, your reckless disregard for consequences led to the loss of liberty, privilege, or prosperity for all concerned. Forced to suppress your high principles and controversial beliefs at the time to obtain freedom, you're now more spiritual, insightful, and risk-taking than you outwardly appear.

With a great sense of humor and divine intuition as your hidden strengths, you're also funnier than we'd guess and a lot luckier than you know. It seems your past search for wisdom and growth has instilled a deep need for both physical excitement and intellectual challenge. No wonder you're never satisfied with your current level of education or certain of your physical limitations. Although lofty aspirations and unrealistic expectations were the cause of your past undoing, apparently they're still available to invoke your present downfall. You unconsciously avoid the freedom and abundance you desire by becoming involved with confining people or restrictive situations. Gambling is your weakness, but self-indulgence is your addiction. Opportunities to obtain higher education or explore new horizons are realized through marriage. Previous experiences and influences include ministry, philosophy, education, exploration, entertainment, law, and adventure. You're surprisingly athletic and secretly judgmental.

Cosmic Advice: You can be right, or you can be happy.

Capricorn in the 12th House: Saturn Rules

Your soul's previous existence was one of material success and public achievement. While your ambitious pursuit of wealth, prestige, and authority was rewarded in this past incarnation, it seems the irresponsible use of power led to serious loss, confinement, or isolation. Forced by guilt to suppress your worldly aspirations, you buried them here in the deadly domain of deep denial. As a result, you are now more conservative than you appear and far more ambitious than you would like to admit. Apparently, the past has left you with an aversion to public scrutiny and a strong preference for working behind the scenes. Not surprisingly, you often unconsciously avoid the recognition and status you deserve by being drawn to dead-end positions, low-profile work, or partners with chronic health issues.

While scandal or public disgrace was the cause of your past undoing, the self-discipline and determination you managed to display at that time are now your hidden strengths. Yes, work is your addiction, but depression is your weakness. Extremely trustworthy in the past, your achievements in this lifetime tend to involve confidential matters or secret projects. You clearly have a karmic connection to your parents and serious issues of loss or deprivation with your father. No wonder you can't get a good night's sleep. Previous influences and experiences include politician, ruler, government service, public administrator, mathematician, engineer, and tycoon. Your unfounded phobias and unconscious guilt are controlling you.

Cosmic Advice: Stop choosing to be alone and then you can stop wondering why you are.

Aquarius in the 12th House: Uranus Rules

Your soul's previous existence was one of humanitarian ideals and creative ingenuity. Committed to the prospect of universal brotherhood and social reform in this past incarnation, you became involved with individuals who stimulated your visionary brilliance and groups that shared your scientific principles. Unfortunately, these radical ideas, revolutionary methods, or unconventional associates provoked irreversible upheaval, which eventually led to extreme loss, exile, or confinement. Overwhelmed by guilt and shame, you suppressed your creative genius and buried your individuality here in the authorized asylum of anonymity. Hence, you are now more independent, inventive, eccentric, and, of course, uncooperative than you appear. It seems your previous effort to embrace the future and evoke change has left you unconsciously resentful of tradition and authority. It has also left you instinctively drawn to anything unique or unorthodox and secretly determined to be different.

Apparently, the innovative and rebellious tendencies that were responsible for your past undoing are still present and accounted for in this lifetime. In fact, your progressive thinking and flashes of brilliant intuition are your hidden strengths. Freedom is your addiction because nonconformity is your weakness. You often unconsciously avoid the close friendships and camaraderie you desire by being drawn to secret societies, clandestine affiliations, and treacherous associates. This explains why you're really a closet maverick who suffers from frequent feelings of loneliness. Previous influences and experiences include astronomer, scientist, inventor, revolutionary, aviator, lecturer, and humanitarian. You have unusual secrets and uncommon spiritual experiences.

Cosmic Advice: Beware of past associates wielding future technology.

Pisces in the 12th House: Neptune Rules

Your soul's previous existence was one of emotional healing and compassionate service. Although helping the less fortunate was your calling in this past incarnation, it seems your profound faith, compassion, or sacrifice led to painful loss or unbearable confinement. Guilt was inflicted—lots of it. As a result, your vulnerabilities were suppressed, which is why you are now more sympathetic, sensitive, and helpful than you outwardly appear. You prefer it that way. Personal privacy is an obsession because protecting your vulnerability is a means of survival. This insufferable past has instilled such a deep aversion to direct confrontation that you now become vague, secretive, and tactically defensive when you think you're being interrogated. While deception or self-pity were definitely the cause of your past undoing, spiritual wisdom and creative imagination are clearly your hidden strengths. Your past martyrdom has left you with a deep need to soften the harsh realities of life and a propensity for altered states of consciousness. We can stop wondering why alcohol, drugs, and fantasy are your escape routes of choice and rose-colored glasses are your addiction. You now unconsciously avoid your mission to rescue others by becoming the victim or dropout yourself. Secluded places near the water have great appeal, while psychic dreams, feelings of guilt, and the forgotten past are often overwhelming. Past influences and experiences include creative arts, music, healing, photography, spirituality, the ocean, and clandestine or illegal activities. You're surprisingly lonely and deathly afraid of confinement.

Cosmic Advice: Get real or get a therapist.

Prologue

What's past is prologue.

—WILLIAM SHAKESPEARE

Now, tell the truth, the next time someone asks you "what's your sign?" what will you say? More importantly, what will you be thinking? Hopefully, it will be smug thoughts about universal degrees and karmic credentials. What about the next time you're getting ready to pay your monthly bills—will you be thinking about your debt to Neptune and worrying about nudges? I hope so. Because, if you are, then my work here is done, which means your hour is up, the session is over, and your soul's suiting up for the game. While my 10th house Sun couldn't be any prouder if that happens, your natal Sun couldn't be any brighter when it does, no matter where it is, because at that very moment, karmic promises are going to start being kept, karmic debts are going to start getting paid, and Saturn's whip is going to stop being cracked over somebody's head. Yes, yours, which is when you'll probably notice that the tide of life is starting to turn a different way. You guessed it, yours. How can you tell? Well, it's not as if you'll be hearing bells or seeing angels the minute you and your soul start reconciling yesterday in the harsh light of today, at least not if you're not hearing or seeing them now. What will happen is that sometime after you do, one of the hard things will feel like it's getting easier, and then a few of the bad things will seem to be getting better. Then the next thing you know, the miserable life you always assumed you were living will suddenly feel like it's getting happier—when in reality, you are. That's a condition that just can't be avoided when your soul's owning up to its promises, you're showing up to keep them, and, together, you're both living up to the contract of your birth chart. So what are you waiting for? Isn't it time you finally became the person you've spent eons preparing to be?

Then it's time to pull out your birth chart and apply what you've learned. If you've learned anything from this book at all, you've learned that there were powerful energies in effect at your birth, and, like you, they had a purpose—not just a physical purpose, but a spiritual purpose as well. Now is the time to make a conscious human effort to live up to the potential of these impressive energies because, according to universal law, when you don't use them wisely you just create worse energies for the next time. What's worse, when you don't use them at all, you just create the same next time—your same next time. Then there you are in the very next life ignoring the very same Sun house calling, avoiding the very same Saturn lesson, neglecting the very same Neptune invoice, and flexing the very same Pluto paranoia that actually put you behind the karmic eight ball in this one. Can you say déjà vu all over again? That's what you're in for when you become the universal no-show who allows your indiscriminate soul to just sign you up for another wheel-spinning lifetime of wasting the brilliant talents you should be developing, succumbing to the fears and inadequacies you should be conquering, falling victim to the emotional addictions from which you should be rescuing others, and choosing automatic weapons to protect yourself from the possibility of intruders when the powerful efficiency of a high-tech security system would do a much better job of keeping you safe—and out of jail. Sound familiar? Of course it does. We can always recognize our selves in the birth chart. With so many deja vu trips under our spiritual belts, our soul's been through it all many times, and there lies the problem. The human part of us gets dragged along for every redundant ride, and the worst thing is, we don't have to, because the best thing is we can do something here in this life to change that dreary cycle if we want to. We can create a different cycle, a less dreary one, a new one. In fact, as just about every psychologist today will tell you, the best predictor of future behavior is past behavior.

If we really do want our soul to take us someplace else on the next earthly journey, all we have to do is make sure it does something else on this one, like finish the journey it started. This journey. That includes keeping the promises, paying the debts, and learning the lessons our soul agreed to. While that means we must consciously let go of all the attitudes and behaviors that didn't work for us in the past, no matter how comfortable they are to the soul, that only serves the higher purpose of making room for the better ones that will work for us in the here and now. That brings us to your own natal Sun's ninety-three-million-mile question: are you ready to keep your powerful rendezvous with the future? Well, then, it's time for your soul to relinquish the past.

That means today is the day to walk into your Sun house, crank up your solar degree, and claim your stardom. Your megawatt life is waiting for you, but then, so is Saturn. Be sure to show up in that classroom not just ready to earn the success you've been guaranteed in this life, but really prepared to learn the 29½-year lesson you've been avoiding since the last one. How long can fame and fortune wait? While there's truly no better time than right now to start paying up what you owe in your Neptune house and no better day to start tapping into the deep reserves in your Pluto arsenal, that's only because there's really no better way for anyone to start making their life better, their world brighter, their soul happier. In fact, wouldn't you say it's time for all of us to change the quality of our lives by just living up to the responsibility of our birth chart? I would, right here and right now, because if we don't, then Shakespeare was right. On this planet, in this world, our past will always be prologue. What happened to us before is bound to happen to us again, and again—and yet again. It has to. After all, according to divine order in general and the universal laws of Oneness, Correspondence, and Compensation in particular, nothing happens by chance. Nothing. This means our life and circumstances will always be a direct result of our own actions or, in many cases, the lack of them. That is why when we do nothing to change today we're really doing nothing but allowing yesterday to become tomorrow, and the next day, and the next year, and the next life. The truth is the minute our soul stops growing, developing, and learning, our future can't be anything but our past because that's when tomorrow can't be anything but yesterday—unless, of course, you now believe as I do that by just applying a little cosmic sense, it really doesn't have to be.

Cosmic Glossary

Contract with the Universe: The interpretation of the natal chart from the soul's perspective.

Cosmic/Universal Law: The principles of divine order that keep the universe from chaos: Oneness, Correspondence, Vibration, Polarity, Rhythm, Compensation, and Gender.

Cosmos: The ever-present, all-knowing, well-ordered universe.

Horoscope: A view of the universal environment at the time of birth. (Greek: *hora* "time" + *skopos* "observer")

Karmic Calling: Where your soul promised you would apply the energies, expertise, and talent of your karmic degree (Sun sign) to become a star. The areas of life represented by your natal Sun house.

Karmic Closet: Your soul's storage unit for painful memories and unbearable experiences. The 12th house of your natal chart.

Karmic Debt: The emotional service you owe to the universe in this life to compensate for your emotional selfishness in a previous one. The areas of life represented by your natal Neptune house.

Karmic Degree: The expertise and skills that were previously earned by the soul and are now yours. The energies of your Sun sign.

Karmic Law: Cause and effect for the soul. The sum of a person's actions in the present existence is what determines the soul's fate in future existences.

Karmic Lesson: The crippling inadequacy you must overcome in this life to achieve material success. The areas of life represented by your natal Saturn house.

Natal/Birth Chart: A diagram of the natal sky that maps the mathematical positions of the planets and constellations at the time of a person's birth.

Natal Sky: The sky as seen from the exact place and at the exact moment of someone's birth.

Neptune Nudge: An overwhelming emotional circumstance that you're pushed into without warning when you're avoiding the emotional service you should be performing.

The 12 Houses of the Birth Chart (and What You Keep in Them)

House 1: Individual Self You Your ego Your physical body/appearance Your physical appearance Your early childhood	**House 5: Individual Creations** Your artistic talent Your creations/artistry/children Your lovers and romantic partners Your recreational pursuits Risks/gambles/investments	**House 9: Far-Reaching Environments** Your beliefs Your advertising/publishing endeavors Your long distance anything Your college education and beyond Your in-laws and distant relatives
House 2: Personal Worth Your personal values Your earning power Your material resources Your money and financial affairs Acquisitions/possessions	**House 6: Daily Life** Your everyday work Your exercise/diet/fitness Your physical health Your physical service to others Your daily practices and routines	**House 10: Career/Society** Your father/authority figures Your professional life and career Your public image and reputation Your ambition/responsibility/success
House 3: Local Environment Your mind Your communications Your local network Your school and education Your siblings and nearby relatives	**House 7: Significant Others** Significant others Your marriages Your partnerships Your adversaries/opponents Your contracts/commitments	**House 11: Social Contributions** Your idealistic visions Your group accomplishments Your friends/associates/peers Your social circle/clubs/associations Your humanitarian endeavors
House 4: Home/Family Your mother/maternal influence Your home life and household Your family and ancestry Real estate/homeland/agriculture	**House 8: Collective Worth** Your deep desires Your emotional power Resources that don't belong to you Your secrets and intimate affairs Your death/legacies/insurance	**House 12: Eternal Life** Your soul Your faith/imagination/spirituality Your mental health Your emotional service to others Your karma and past lives

To Write to the Author

If you wish to contact the author or would like more information about this book, please write to the author in care of Llewellyn Worldwide and we will forward your request. Both the author and publisher appreciate hearing from you and learning of your enjoyment of this book and how it has helped you. Llewellyn Worldwide cannot guarantee that every letter written to the author can be answered, but all will be forwarded. Please write to:

Marguerite Manning
℅ Llewellyn Worldwide
2143 Wooddale Drive, Dept. 978-0-7387-1054-9
Woodbury, Minnesota 55125-2989, U.S.A.

Please enclose a self-addressed stamped envelope for reply, or $1.00 to cover costs. If outside the U.S.A., enclose international postal reply coupon.

Many of Llewellyn's authors have websites with additional information and resources. For more information, please visit our website at http://www.llewellyn.com.

Free Catalog

Get the latest information on our body, mind, and spirit products! To receive a **free** copy of Llewellyn's consumer catalog, *New Worlds of Mind & Spirit,* simply call 1-877-NEW-WRLD or visit our website at www.llewellyn.com and click on *New Worlds.*

Llewellyn Ordering Information

Order Online:

Visit our website at www.llewellyn.com, select your books, and order them on our secure server.

Order by Phone:

- Call toll-free within the U.S. at 1-877-NEW-WRLD (1-877-639-9753). Call toll-free within Canada at 1-866-NEW-WRLD (1-866-639-9753)
- We accept VISA, MasterCard, and American Express

Order by Mail:

Send the full price of your order (MN residents add 6.5% sales tax) in U.S. funds, plus postage & handling to:

Llewellyn Worldwide
2143 Wooddale Drive, Dept. 978-0-7387-1054-9
Woodbury, MN 55125-2989

Postage & Handling:

Standard (U.S., Mexico, & Canada). If your order is:
$24.99 and under, add $3.00
$25.00 and over, FREE STANDARD SHIPPING

AK, HI, PR: $15.00 for one book plus $1.00 for each additional book.

International Orders (airmail only):
$16.00 for one book plus $3.00 for each additional book

Orders are processed within 2 business days.
Please allow for normal shipping time. Postage and handling rates subject to change.

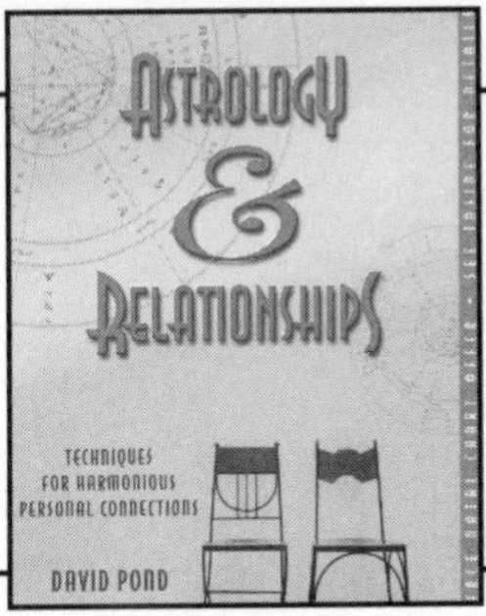

Astrology & Relationships

Techniques for Harmonious Personal Connections

David Pond

Take your relationships to a deeper level. There is a hunger for intimacy in the modern world. *Astrology & Relationships* is a guidebook on how to use astrology to improve all your relationships. This is not fortunetelling astrology, predicting which signs you will be most compatible with; instead, it uses astrology as a model to help you experience greater fulfillment and joy in relating to others. You can also look up your planets, and those of others, to discover specific relationship needs and talents.

What makes this book unique is that it goes beyond descriptive astrology to suggest methods and techniques for actualizing the stages of a relationship that each planet represents. Many of the exercises are designed to awaken individual skills and heighten self-understanding, leading you to first identify a particular quality within yourself, and then to relate to it in others.

0-7387-0046-0, 416 pp., 7½ x 9⅛ **$21.95**

To order, call 1-877-NEW-WRLD

Prices subject to change without notice

Astrology

Understanding the Birth Chart

(A Comprehensive Guide to Classical Interpretation)

Kevin Burk

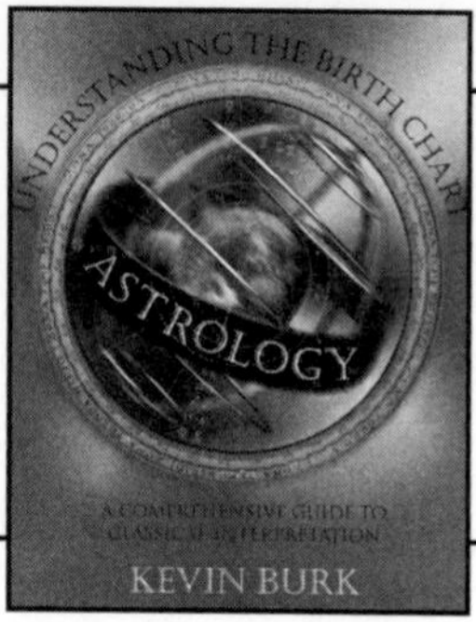

This beginning- to intermediate-level astrology book is based on a course taught to prepare students for the NCGR Level I Astrological Certification exam. It is a unique book for several reasons. First, rather than being an astrological phrase book or "cookbook," it helps students to understand the language of astrology. From the beginning, students are encouraged to focus on the concepts, not the keywords. Second, as soon as you are familiar with the fundamental elements of astrology, the focus shifts to learning how to work with these basics to form a coherent, synthesized interpretation of a birth chart.

In addition, it explains how to work with traditional astrological techniques, most notably the essential dignities. All interpretive factors are brought together in the context of a full interpretation of the charts of Sylvester Stallone, Meryl Streep, Eva Peron, and Woody Allen. This book fits the niche between cookbook astrology books and more technical manuals.

1-56718-088-4, 368 pp., 7½ x 9⅛, illus. **$17.95**

TO ORDER, CALL 1-877-NEW-WRLD

PRICES SUBJECT TO CHANGE WITHOUT NOTICE

The Ex Files

A Zodiac Guide to His Former Flames

ROWAN DAVIS

If your guy's ex is driving you crazy, check out this fun astrological guide to figuring her out.

Blending the wisdom of the stars with tension-lifting humor, Rowan Davis takes an honest look at an unpleasant part of life—dealing with your man's ex. From vengeful Leos to secretive Scorpios, *The Ex Files* dishes the dirt on all twelve Sun signs and gives insight into what you can expect from each. There's also candid advice—based on your own Sun sign—for coping with a variety of exes. Learn how to ignore the scare tactics of the Aries . . . wise up to the Pisces' emotional games . . . and see through the Aquarius' ploy to win him back. And for those who want to take action, you can find out which signs are open to friendship, could use discouragement, or are best left alone.

0-7387-1044-X, 216 pp., 5 x 6 **$12.95**

TO ORDER, CALL 1-877-NEW-WRLD

PRICES SUBJECT TO CHANGE WITHOUT NOTICE

Houses

A Contemporary Guide

GWYNETH BRYAN

Blending astrology, psychology, and metaphor, this astrological guide helps readers grasp the dynamics of each of the twelve astrological houses. Humor and personal anecdotes bring astrological concepts—such as the Ascendant, Descendant, Midheaven, and the Nadir—to life. The astrological birth charts of Bill Clinton, Gloria Steinem, Donald Trump, Martha Stewart, George W. Bush, and other important icons are used as colorful examples to demonstrate how the planets within each house can influence childhood, physical appearance, personality, career, relationships, spiritual growth, and other aspects of life.

Gwyneth Bryan is an astrology consultant and teacher, as well as a second level Reiki practitioner. She is a founding member of the South Jersey Jung Seminar and Inner Workshop and long-time member of the Association for Research and Enlightenment in Virginia. An award-winning arts reporter and critic for a New Jersey magazine, she has also written for the *Philadelphia Inquirer, Prevention*, New Jersey Life, New Frontier, and other publications.

0-7387-0868-2, 192 pp., 7½ x 9⅛ **$14.95**

TO ORDER, CALL 1-877-NEW-WRLD

PRICES SUBJECT TO CHANGE WITHOUT NOTICE

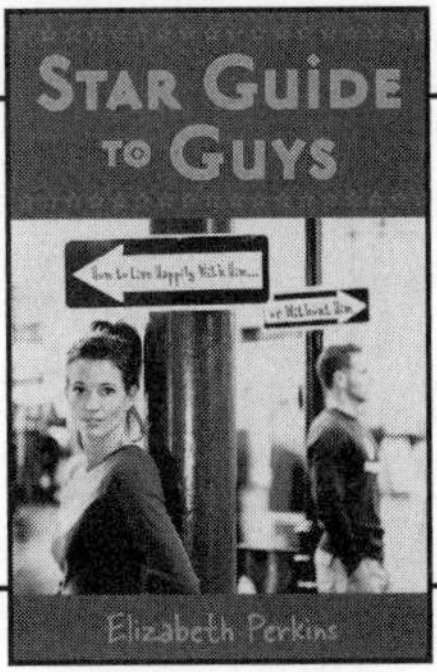

Star Guide to Guys

How to Live Happily With Him . . . or Without Him

ELIZABETH PERKINS

Is your hot yoga instructor a high-strung Virgo or a sensitive Pisces? Could the cutie in the coffee shop be the Leo of your dreams? Thanks to astrology, women can get the nitty-gritty on a crush before leaping into the murky depths of a relationship.

The Star Guide to Guys dishes out the lowdown on men in all twelve sun signs—covering their strengths, challenges, goals, desires, and other personality traits. Women can also depend on this entertaining, easy-to-use guide for insight into their own sign: what they're looking for in a mate, relationship needs, and dynamic compatibility with each sign. For ladies on a break from the dating scene, there's also astrological advice for living a fabulous single life and loving it.

0-7387-0954-9, 240 pp., 6 x 9 **$12.95**

TO ORDER, CALL 1-877-NEW-WRLD

PRICES SUBJECT TO CHANGE WITHOUT NOTICE

The New A TO Z Horoscope Maker and Delineator

LLEWELLYN GEORGE

A textbook . . . encyclopedia . . . self-study course . . . and extensive astrological dictionary all in one! More American astrologers have learned their craft from *The New A to Z Horoscope and Delineator* than any other astrology book.

First published in 1910, it is in every sense a complete course in astrology, giving beginners all the basic techniques and concepts they need to get off on the right foot. Plus it offers the more advanced astrologer an excellent dictionary and reference work for calculating and analyzing transits, progression, rectifications, and creating locality charts. This new edition has been revised to meet the needs of the modern audience.

0-7387-322-2, 480 pp., 7½ x 9⅛ **$22.95**

TO ORDER, CALL 1-877-NEW-WRLD

PRICES SUBJECT TO CHANGE WITHOUT NOTICE

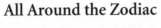

All Around the Zodiac

Exploring Astrology's Twelve Signs

Bil Tierney

A fresh, in-depth perspective on the zodiac you thought you knew. This book provides a revealing new look at the astrological signs, from Aries to Pisces. Gain a deeper understanding of how each sign motivates you to grow and evolve in consciousness. How does Aries work with Pisces? What does Gemini share in common with Scorpio? *All Around the Zodiac* is the only book on the market to explore these sign combinations to such a degree.

Not your typical Sun sign guide, this book is broken into three parts. Part 1 defines the signs, part 2 analyzes the expression of sixty-six pairs of signs, and part 3 designates the expression of the planets and houses in the signs.

0-7387-0111-4, 528 pp., 6 x 9 **$21.95**

To order, call 1-877-NEW-WRLD

Prices subject to change without notice